Eighteenth Century Bibliographies

Handlists of Critical Studies Relating to Smollett,
Richardson, Sterne, Fielding, Dibdin,
18th Century Medicine, the 18th Century Novel,
Godwin, Gibbon, Young, and Burke.
To which is added John P. Anderson's Bibliography of Smollett.

by

Francesco Cordasco

The Scarecrow Press, Inc.
Metuchen, N.J.   1970

Copyright 1947, 1948, 1950, 1952, 1970
by Francesco Cordasco

SBN 8108-0288-0

Table of Contents

Page

	Introduction	
I	Smollett Criticism, 1770-1924. A Bibliography Enumerative and Annotative....................	7
II	Smollett Criticism, 1925-1945. A Compilation.....	39
III	Samuel Richardson. A List of Critical Studies Published from 1896-1946.	55
IV	Laurence Sterne. A List of Critical Studies Published from 1895-1946.....................	73
V	Henry Fielding. A List of Critical Studies Published from 1895-1946.....................	93
VI	A Bibliography of Thomas Frognall Dibdin, Author of the Bibliomania.....................	119
VII	An Introduction to 18th Century Medical Bibliography. With a Handlist of Medical References and Bibliographies Published in the 18th Century.	133
VIII	The 18th Century Novel. A Handlist of General Histories and Articles of the Last Twenty-Five Years with a Notice of Bibliographical Guides. With an Introductory Note by Professor James R. Foster.	145
IX	William Godwin: A Handlist of Critical Notices and Studies................................	167
X	Edward Gibbon: A Handlist of Critical Notices and Studies................................	175
XI	Edward Young: A Handlist of Critical Notices and Studies.	183
XII	Edmund Burke: A Handlist of Critical Notices and Studies................................	191
XIII	A Bibliography of Smollett by John P. Anderson...	207

Introduction

In the late 1940's, Long Island University Press published an 18th century bibliographical series which was edited by the late Tristram Walker Metcalfe and which I compiled. (18th Century Bibliographical Pamphlets, Numbers 1-12, Brooklyn: Long Island University Press, 1947-50). The Series was on representative authors in belles-lettres, science, and history; with certain issues to be given to general bibliography. In the twenty-odd years which have passed, the pamphlets (which have been out of print for years) have been very difficult to obtain, and very few libraries have complete sets. Their value is attested to not only by the many continuing requests in antiquarian journals, but also by their recurrent listing as important bibliographical resources, e.g., most recently in T. H. Howard Hill, ed., Bibliography of British Literary Bibliographies (Oxford University Press, 1969). It is to meet this continuing need, and to make the pamphlets more easily accessible that they are now gathered together and published in this volume. Together, the pamphlets list over 1300 main references, with additional notices of several hundred reviews and other titles in the annotations. In this reprinting, I have made no changes and have retained the prefaces to each of the pamphlets.

The major continuing references for 18th century bibliography are the annual bibliographies published since 1926 in the Philological Quarterly, and which have been brought together in English Literature 1660-1800 [vol. I: 1926-1938; vol. II: 1939-1950; vol. III: 1951-1956; vol. IV: 1957-1960], Princeton: Princeton University Press, 1950-1962. Robert Watt's monumental Bibliotheca Britannica (Edinburgh: Archibald Constable, 1824. 4 vols.) has been republished, and along with William Thomas Lowndes' The Bibliographer's Manual (London: Henry G. Bohn, 1857-1864. 10 vols.), also recently republished, afford great bibliographical resources for 18th century study.[1] Attention should be drawn to important reviews of the pamphlets: Fielding, in Philological Quarterly, vol. 29 (July 1950), pp. 273-275; and Richardson, in Philological Quarterly, vol. 29 (July 1950), pp. 294-295; and to Paul G. Boucé, "Smollett

Criticism," <u>Notes & Queries</u>, vol. CCXII (1967), pp. 184-187 which makes important corrections and additions.

The reissue of the pamphlets has allowed the opportunity to add the valuable bibliography of Smollett compiled by John P. Anderson, of the British Museum staff, which was appended to David Hannay's <u>Life of Tobias George Smollett</u> (London: Walter Scott, 1887).

F. C.
May 1969

Notes

See F. Cordasco, "British Bibliographical Monument: Robert Watt's <u>Bibliotheca Britannica</u>," <u>Library Journal</u>, vol. 90 (Sept. 15, 1965), pp. 3584-3585; and F. Cordasco, "William Thomas Lowndes and The Bibliographer's Manual: A Retrospective Essay," /London/ <u>Library Association Record</u>, October, 1968, pp. 263-265.

I.

Smollett Criticism, 1770-1924:
a Bibliography, Enumerative and Annotative

Copyright 1948 by Francesco Cordasco

Preface

There must be a good reason for a bibliography today. Too often the individual who has been trained in literature (whatever that may entail) becomes, instead of critic or creator, a statistician, bibliographer, or hoary antiquarian laboriously elucidating the most trivial detail; and this examination of peripheria, most times, at the expense of a lifetime. The profession of letters is obviously the demonstration of the vitality of the literature examined: its philosophical strata, its relation to human history, and its concurrency in human ideas. We need more of the omniscence of George Saintsbury, more criticism with grasp, avec profondeur, less of the dry-rot which, unendingly, gluts the presses of the professional journals. It is with these sentiments that the writer tenders this compilation. Apologetically, it serves only to afford access to the materials consulted by the compiler in the more important organization of a biography of Tobias George Smollett and an examination of his times. The writer is comforted in the realization that the compilation will afford the most complete bibliographic guide, but that comfort is not justification for its publication.

The structure of the list needs clarification. We have not attempted a bibliography of the Works for two reasons: 1) the collation of texts, and the enumeration of editions are the work of the literary statistician, and only limitedly assume critical importance; 2) Miss L. F. Norwood has announced this statistical domain, virtute propria illustris, her own (see CBEL, II, 523). The opening date has been chosen to avoid the notice of contemporary reputation which well affords for another study. Terminally, 1924 has seemed advisable since, from that date forward, materials are easily available (see # 5). The chronological limitations of the study have not been observed in I. Bibliography for the good reason that the items therein listed supplement the actual compilation. Every care has been taken to avoid errors.

Particular thanks are due Professor James R. Foster, good Smollettian, Mr. Elliot S. M. Gatner, Mr. Nathan

Resnick, and Mr. Milton Cohen for valuable suggestions. To Señor Miguel Rámon Madorma, who so happily combines the professions of medicine and letters, and to whom Smollett has ever been a joy, gratitude is due for the perusal of materials not available to the writer.

F. C.

Contents

I.	Bibliography.	13
II.	Biography and General Criticism.	14
III.	Plays and Poems.	33
IV.	Translations.	34
V.	Historical Writings.	34
VI.	History and Adventures of an Atom.	35
VII.	Travels through France and Italy.	35
VIII.	Adventures of Roderick Random.	35
IX.	Adventures of Peregrine Pickle.	36
X.	Adventures of Ferdinand, Count Fathom.	37
XI.	Adventures of Sir Launcelot Greaves.	37
XII.	The Expedition of Humphry Clinker.	37

Smollett Criticism, 1770-1924: a Bibliography,
Enumerative and Annotative.

I. Bibliography

Anderson, John P., in David Hannay, Life of Tobias   1.
   George Smollett, London, 1887. Appendix, pp.
   i-x.
   The fullest bibliography available.

Baker, Ernest A., The history of the English novel: 2.
   intellectual realism from Richardson to Sterne,
   London, 1930.
   Brief bibliography, pp. 279-280.

Black, G. F., Bulletin, New York Public Library,   3.
   XVIII (Dec. 1914), pp. 1561-2.

Boege, Fred W., Smollett's reputation as a novelist,   4.
   Princeton University press, 1947. A selective
   bibliography, pp. 150-168.

Cordasco, F., Smollett criticism, 1925-1945: a   5.
   compilation, Brooklyn, 1947.
   Lists 73 items.

Drinker, Cecil K., "Doctor Smollett," Annals of   6.
   Medical History, VII (March 1925), pp. 31-47.
   Bibliography, 46-47.

Isaacs, J. H., in Roderick Random, Peregrine Pickle,   7.
   and Humphry Clinker, London, 1895.

Joliat, Eugène, Smollett et la France, Paris, 1935.   8.
   Bibliothèque de la Revue de littérature comparée #105.
   Bibliography of European translations, pp. 255-
   69. General bibliography, pp. 270-74.

Jones, Claude E., Smollett studies (University of   9.
   California publications in English, IX, #2)
   Berkeley, 1942.

Bibliography, pp. 129-133. Particular reference to Smollett's connexions with the Critical Review and the navy.

10. Nangle, B. C., The Monthly Review, indexes of contributors and articles, Oxford, 1934.
Smollet's contributions, p. 42.

11. Norwood, L. F., "Tobias George Smollett," in Cambridge bibliography of English literature, New York, 1941, II, pp. 523-527.
A selective list of items in #1, #3, #7, #13

12. _____: A bibliography of the works of Tobias Smollett [in preparation].
Information unavailable.

13. Noyes, Edward S., The letters of Tobias Smollett, Harvard University Press, Cambridge, 1926.
Bibliography, pp. 237-241.

14. Tobin, James E., Eighteenth century literature and its cultural background: a bibliography, New York, Fordham University Press, 1939.
Bibliography, pp. 157-158.

15. Seccombe, T., "Smollett," Dictionary of national biography.
Brief bibliography appended.

II. Biography and General Criticism

16. All the year round, LXVIII (1891), pp. 420-24.
"Smollett in the South."

17. Allibone, S. Austin, A critical dictionary of English literature, Phila., 1899. 3v.; II, 2165-2167.
A general commentary.

18. Almon, John, Correspondence of John Wilkes, London, 1805. 5v.
Letters of Smollett to Wilkes, I, pp. 49-51.
See Horace Bleackley, Life of John Wilkes, London, 1917.

19. American quarterly review, XVI (1834), pp. 503-504.
Smollett and Fielding. See #195.

Smollett Criticism, 1770-1924.   15

Anderson, Robert, Life of Tobias George Smollett,   20.
  Edinburgh, 1803.
  See #21.

————— : Miscellaneous works of Tobias George   21.
  Smollett, Edinburgh, 1796. 6v.
  Six editions by 1820; memoir of Smollett (ed.
  1820) pp. 1-203. The life originally appeared
  in Anderson's edition, Works of the British
  poets, Edinburgh, 1795.

Anderson, William, The Scottish nation; or the sur-   22.
  names, families, literature, honours, and biographical history of the people of Scotland,
  Edinburgh, 1863. 3v.
  Notices of Smollett, III, pp. 483-485; portrait.

Anglo-Italian review, IV (1919), pp. 31-45.   23.
  Smollett in Italy.

Anglo-Saxon review, IX (1901), pp. 123-138.   24.
  A general article.

The Athenaeum, December 8, 1888, pp. 767-769.   25.
  A review of #109.

Barbauld, Mrs., The British novelists, London,   26.
  1810, 50v.
  "Introduction," XXX. Unfavorable notices.

Beattie, James, Dissertations moral and critical,   27.
  Dublin, 1783. 2v.
  II, pp. 316-317.

Becker, Gustav, "Die Bedeutung des Wortes romantic   28.
  bei Fielding und Smollett," Archiv für das
  Studium der Neueren Sprachen und Literaturen,
  CX (1903), pp. 56-66.

The Bee or literary intelligencer, VIII (1792), p. 316. 29.
  Smollett and literature of Scotland. See
  #141, #144.

The Bee, VII (1795), pp. 130-132.   30.
  A commentary on the novels.

Beljame, Alexandre, Le public et les hommes de   31.

lettres en Angleterre au dixhuitième siècle, Paris, 1881.

Binz-Winiger, E., Erziehungsfragen in den Romanen von Richardson, Fielding, Smollett, Goldsmith und Sterne, Zurich, 1924.   32.

Biographical magazine, I (1794), pp. unnumbered.   33.
Brief biographical notice.

Bisset, Robert, The historical, biographical, literary and scientific magazine, I (1798), pp. 55-56.   34.
A preference for Fielding. See # 195.

Blackwood's Edinburgh magazine, XV (1824), pp. 407-408; 414.   35.
Smollett and Scott. See # 200.

Ibid., CLXIV (1898), p. 231.   36.
Smollett and the old sea-dogs.

Ibid., CLXVII (1900), pp. 697-699.   37.
Review of # 115. See # 44.

Bookman, March (1906), pp. 241-243.   38.
General commentary on the novels.

British critic, XII (1798), pp. 59-60.   39.
A notice and review of # 21.

British medical journal, I, January 3 (1903), pp. 40-41.   40.
"Doctors in British fiction."

The British Plutarch, containing the lives of the most eminent statesmen... 3rd ed., London, 1791. 8v.   41.
A notice of Smollett; VIII, pp. 117-128.

British review, XI (1818), pp. 40-42.   42.
Unfavorable notice of Smollett.

Brydges, Samuel E., Censuria literaria, London, 1805-09. 10v.   43.
IV, 81; an attack.

Burton, Richard, "The vigorous Dr. Smollett," Dial,   44.

Smollett Criticism, 1770-1924.   17

XXXII (1902), pp. 81-83.
A review of #115. See #37.

Carlyle, Alexander, Autobiography, ed. J. H. Burton,   45.
   Edinburgh, 1860.
   Carlyle was an acquaintance of Smollett;
   See #13 for exchange of letters.

Chambers, Robert, Smollett, his life, and a selec-   46.
   tion from his writings, London, 1867.

_____, Traditions of Edinburgh, London, 1869.   47.
   Smollett's visit to Edinburgh.

_____, Biographical dictionary of eminent   48.
   Scotsmen, new ed., London, 1870. 5v.

Chambers, William, Memoir of Robert Chambers,   49.
   New York, 1872.
   See pp. 54-55; 95 in connection with #46.

Chancellor, E. B., "Tobias Smollett," Chamber's   50.
   Journal, XI (1921), pp. 241-244.

_____, "Smollett as traveller," Fortnightly   51.
   review, new series, CVIII, pp. 478-488.

Chandler, F. W., Literature of roguery, New York,   52.
   1907. 2v.

Charles, Phelarète, Le XVIIIe siècle en Angleterre,   53.
   Paris, 1846. 2v.
   See II, pp. 369-371

Child, Harold, "Fielding and Smollett," Cambridge   54.
   history of English literature, X, New York,
   1913. See #195.

Clarke, C. C., "On the comic writers of England,"   55.
   Gentleman's magazine, new series, VIII
   (1872), pp. 565-575. Same as #98.

Craig, N. B., Memoirs of Major Robert Stobo,   56.
   Pittsburgh, 1854.
   Stobo was an acquaintance of Smollett and
   may have been the model for Lieutenant
   Lismahago.

Creech, William, Edinburgh fugitive pieces, 57.
   Edinburgh, 1815.
   Unfavorable notices; see pp. 155, 277, 342.

Critical review, LX (1785), p. 58. 58.
   An answer to Clara Reeve's strictures.
   See #206.

Ibid., LXV (1788), p. 130. 59.
   Imitations of Smollett noted.

Ibid., LXVII (1789), p. 76. 60.
   Imitations of Smollett noted.

Ibid., 2nd series, I (1791), p. 470. 61.
   Imitations of Smollett noted.

Ibid., 2nd series, II (1791), pp. 233, 356. 62.
   General criticism.

Ibid., 2nd series, XXII (1798), pp. 357-358. 63.
   Imitations of Smollett noted.

Ibid., 2nd series, XXIII (1798) p. 472. 64.
   Imitations of Smollett noted.

Ibid., 2nd series, XXX (1800), p. 230. 65.
   Imitations of Smollett noted.

Cross, W. L., Development of the English novel, 66.
   New York, 1904.

_____ "Smollett - two centuries after," 67.
   Literary review, I, May 14, (1921).

Cruikshank, George, Illustrations of Smollett, 68.
   Fielding, and Goldsmith, in a series of
   41 plates, designed and engraved by
   George Cruikshank, accompanied by descriptive extracts, London, 1832.

Davis, William, A second journey round the library 69.
   of a bibliomaniac, London, 1825.
   Key to Adventures of an atom, pp. 115-118.

Dibelius, Wilhelm, Englische Romankunst. Die 70.
   technik des englischen Romans in

Smollett Criticism, 1770-1924.   19

achtzehnten und zu anfang des neunzehnten
Jahrhunderts, Berlin, 1910.
See Journal of English and Germanic
philology, II (1912), pp. 626-635.

De Quincey, Thomas, Works, Riverside edition,   71.
   New York, 1876-77. 12v.
   See adverse criticism, III, pp. 617-18;
   V. p. 348.

D'Israeli, Issac, Essay on the manners and genius   72.
   of the literaty character, London, 1795.
   See p. 140.

Drake, Nathan, Literary hours: or sketches critical, 73.
   narrative and poetical, 4th ed., London,
   1820. 3v.
   I, p. 274. Smollett's Gothic effects.
   See #286, #287.

Duffield, P. "Smollett" in Warner's library of the   74.
   world's best literature, XXIII, p. 13575,
   n.p.; n.d.

Dunlop, John, History of fiction, Phila., 1842,   75.
   (first ed. 1814). 2v.
   II, p. 407 ff.

Edinburgh magazine, or literary miscellany, IV   76.
   (1786), p. 424.
   Smollett and literature of Scotland.

Edinburgh review, XIII (1803), p. 356.   77.
   Smollett abused by Warburton.

Ibid., XXIV (1814), pp. 328-330.   78.
   A commentary on the novels.

Ibid., XXV (1815), p. 483.   79.
   The pleasantry of Smollett.

Ibid., XXIX (1819), p. 209.   80.
   Smollett's residence at Nice.
   See #198.

Ibid., LXVIII (1838), p. 76.   81.
   Smollett and Dickens. See #81, #201.

Ibid., CXIII (1865), p. 167. 82.
    Character of Smollett.

Ibid., CXXI (1873), p. 319. 83.
    A commentary on Taine's strictures.
    See #229.

English review, II (1783), p. 92. 84.
    James Beattie and Hugh Blair: detractors
    of Smollett. See #27.

European magazine, XIX (1791), p. 94. 85.
    A biographic sketch.

Ibid., XXXIII (1798), pp. 100-104. 86.
    A notice and review of #21.

Ibid., LXXVI (1819), p. 512. 87.
    Smollett's grave at Leghorn. See #96.

Filon, Augustin, Histoire de la littérature anglaise. 88.
    Paris, 1883.
    Unfavorable criticism.

Fischer, A., Autobiographisches in Smolletts 89.
    Humphry Clinker, Coburg, 1913.

Ford, D., Admiral Vernon and the navy, London, 90.
    1907.
    Vernon led the ill-fated expedition to Cartagena.

Forster, John, Life of Goldsmith, new ed., London 91.
    1903.
    Numerous references to Smollett.

Forsyth, W., Novels and novelists of the eighteenth 92.
    century, London, 1871.
    See pp. 278-303.

Galli, I., Le réalisme pittoresque chez Le Sage et 93.
    ses prédécesseurs immédiats, Grenoble,
    1910.

Garden, Francis (Lord Gardenstone), Miscellanies in 94.
    prose and verse, 2nd ed., Edinburgh, 1792.
    Verse tributes to Smollett; pp. 103; 222-223.

Smollett Criticism, 1770-1924. 21

General magazine, III (1789), p. 362. 95.
    Imitators of Smollett.

Gentleman's magazine, LXXXVIII (1818), p. 267. 96.
    Smollett's tomb at Leghorn. Cf. #87.

Ibid., XCVI (1826), p. 531. 97.
    Smollett at Nice, Cf. #80.

Ibid., entirely new series, VIII (1872), pp. 565-575. 98.
    Smollett and Fielding, Cf. #19, #32, #34, #54, #99.

Ibid., entirely new series, XIV (1875), pp. 729-737. 99.
    Smollett and Fielding. See #98.

Glascock, William N., Naval sketch book, London, 1834. 2v. 100.
    See chapter, "Strictures of Smollett."

Glaister, J. G., Dr. William Smellie and his contemporaries, Glasgow, 1894. 101.
    Smollett's revision of Smellie's Cases on midwifery.

Godwin, William, "Essay on prose style" in Enquirer, London, 1797. 102.
    See pp. 467-468.

Gosse, Edmund, History of Eighteenth century literature, London, 1888. 103.
    See pp. 258-264.

Graham, H. G., Scottish men of letters in the XVIIIth century, Edinburgh, 1908. 104.

Graham's magazine, XX (1842), p. 187. 105.
    Some commentary by Poe.

Grant, James, Cassell's old and new Edinburgh, London, 1882, 3v. 106.
    References to Smollett.

Green, Robert, "Tobias Smollett, physician and novelist," Boston medical and surgical journal, CLXXI (1914), pp. 635-638. 107.

Habel, U. Die Nachwirkung des picaresken Romans 108.
in England, von Nash bis Fielding und
Smollett, Breslau, 1924 (again 1930).

Hannay, David, Life of Tobias George Smollett, 109.
London, 1887.
Perhaps the best life; see #1, #25.

Happel, F., Tobias Smollett und der Humor, 110.
Marburg, 1910.

Hazlitt, William, Lectures on the English comic 111.
writers, London, 1819.
See pp. 229-233.

_____, Works, ed. P. P. Howe, London and 112.
Toronto, 1933. 21v.
See IV, p. 138; VI, pp. 115-117, 127;
VII, pp. 37, 194; IX, p. 140; X, p. 60;
XII, pp. 36, 303; XVII, pp. 101, 161, 184;
XVIII, pp. 245-246; XX, p. 58.

Heidler, J. B., History, from 1700-1800, of 113.
English criticism of prose fiction, Urbana
(Illionis), s. d.

Henderson, Andrew, A second letter to Samuel 114.
Johnson... with an impartial character of
Dr. Smollett, London 1775.

Henley, W. E., and Seccombe, T., Works of 115.
Tobias Smollett, London, 1899-1902. 12v.
See #37, #44.

Herbert, David, Works of Tobias George Smollett, 116.
Edinburgh, 1870. Memoir, pp. 7-40.

Hillard, George S., Six months in Italy, London, 117.
1853. 2v.
See II, pp. 295-298.

Hunt, Leigh, Correspondence, ed. by eldest son, 118.
London, 1862. 2v.
See I, pp. 80-81, 148; II, p. 83.

Intermédiaire des chercheurs et curieux, (1864), 119.
pp. 308, 364-365.

An answer to Taine's strictures; see
83, # 229.

Irving, J., Some account of the family of   120.
    Smollett of Bonhill; with a series of
    letters hitherto unpublished, written by
    Dr. Smollett, Dumbarton, 1859.

———, The book of Dumbartonshire: a   121.
    history of the county, burghs, parishes,
    and lands, memoirs of families, and
    notices of industries carried on in the
    Lennox district, Edinburgh, 1879. 3v.
    Family of Smollett of Bonhill, II,
    pp. 175-208.

Jackson, Holbrook, Great English novelists,   122.
    London, 1908.

Jeaffreson, J. Cordy, Novels and novelists from   123.
    Elizabeth to Victoria, London, 1858. 2v.
    See I, pp. 148-179.

Knickerbocker magazine, II (1833), p. 315.   124.
    A favorable notice of a 2v. ed. of Smollett
    in Phila.

Lang, Andrew, Adventures among books, London,   125.
    1905.
    Chapter on Smollett.

Lanier, Sydney, The English novel, New York, 1900.   126.
    See pp. 185-188. For Lanier, Smollett
    was "the third so-called classic author."

Legouis, E., and Cazamian, L., Histoire de la   127.
    littérature anglaise, Paris, 1924.
    See pp. 838-842.

L'Estrange, A. G., History of English humour,   128.
    London, 1877. 2v.
    See II, pp. 123-125.

Leuschel, M. F., Autobiographisches in Smolletts   129.
    Roderick Random, Leipzig, 1903.

130. Literary gazette, V (1817), p. 69.
An answer to the unfavorable criticism of
E. S. Barrett, in Six weeks at Longs,
London, 1817.

131. Ibid., LXXXVI (1818), p. 591.
Smollett's grave at Leghorn.
See #87, #96.

132. Living age, February (1892), pp. 507-510.
Smollett in South of Europe, Cf. #16.

133. London magazine, II (1876), pp. 98-103.
Smollett at Chelsea.

134. Lücker, H., Die Verwendung der Mundart in englischen Roman des XVIII Jahrhunderts, Darmstadt, 1915.

135. Mackintosh, James, Memoirs, ed. R. J. Mackintosh, London, 1835. 2v.
See II, pp. 104-105.

136. Mangin, Edward, An essay on light reading, London, 1808. A violent attack on Smollett; see pp. 21-23, 30-31, 46.

137. Masson, David, British novelists and their styles; being a critical sketch of British prose fiction, Cambridge, 1859.
Smollett, pp. 104-107; Fielding and Smollett, pp. 128-145. See #98.

138. Maynadier, G. H., Works of Tobias Smollett, New York, 1902. 12v.
Introductions to the novels.

139. Mézières, Louis, Histoire critique de la littérature anglaise, Paris, 1834. 2v.
See II, pp. 161, 174, 199, 202, 217.

140. Mills, Abraham, The literature and the literary men of Great Britain and Ireland, New York, 1851. 2v.
See II, 514-515.

141. The Mirror, #83 (February 22, 1780).
Smollett and the literature of Scotland.
See #144.

142. Montagu, Mary W., The letters and works of Lady M. W. Montagu, London, 1861. 2v.
References to Smollett.

143. Monthly chronicle, I (1838), p. 50.
"Art in fiction."

144. Monthly magazine, IV (1797), p. 360.
Smollett and literature of Scotland.
See #141.

145. Ibid., IV (1797), pp. 180-181.
Smollett and Richardson.
See #32, #238.

146. Monthly mirror, II (1796), p. 85.
Imitations of Smollett.

147. Monthly review, LVII (1777), p. 142.
Some notices of Smollett's influence.

148. Ibid., LXXIII (1785), p. 418.
Clara Reeve's notice of Smollett in her Progress of Romance.
See #58, #206.

149. Ibid., LXV (1811), p. 418.
Washington Irving and Smollett.
See #196.

150. Moore, John, The works of Tobias Smollet, M.D., London, 1797. 8v.
"A view of the commencement and progress of romance," pp. v-xcv; "Life of Tobias Smollett," pp. xcvii-cxcvi.

151. Mudford, William, ed., British novelists; comprising every work of acknowledged merit which is usually classed under denomination of novels, London, 1810-1816. 5v.
See I, ii, 6; II, iii.

Murphy, Arthur, Life of David Garrick, Dublin, 152.
    1801.
    See pp. 203-204; praise for the humor of
    Smollett.

Murray, Hugh, Morality of fiction, London, 1817. 153.
    See pp. 106 ff.

Nathan, George Jean, "Brookworms of the sea," 154.
    Bookman, XXIX (July 1909), pp. 483-485.

New novelist's magazine, I (1787), pp. 24-27. 155.
    Ascription of "The unfortunate lovers" to
    Smollett.

Newman, Jeremiah, Lounger's common-place book, 156.
    London, 1805. 3v.
    See III, p. 191.

Nicklin, J. A., "An 18th century saga," 157.
    Gentleman's magazine, CCLXXX (1896),
    pp. 453-458.

Nicoll, Henry J., Landmarks of English literature, 158.
    New York, 1883.
    See pp. 222, 224, 228.

Nicols, J., Literary anecdotes of the XVIIIth 159.
    century, London, 1812-16. 9v.
    Numerous references to Smollett.

Nineteenth century, V, (1879), p. 30. 160.
    An article by Trollope on the early
    novelists.

North American review, XXXII (1831), pp. 404- 161.
    405.
    General criticism on the novels.

Ibid., XXXV (1832), pp. 188-189. 162.
    Smollett and Scott. See #200.

Ibid., XXXIX (1834), p. 171. 163.
    Smollett's nastiness.

Ibid., LXIX (1849), p. 386. 164.
    Smollett's virtues.

165. Northumberland and Newcastle magazine, I (1818), p. 247.
"Vicious influence of Smollett."

166. Notes and queries, 2nd series, III, April 25 (1857), p. 326. Letters from Dr. Smollett to Dr. Armstrong.

167. Ibid., 2nd series, XII, July 20 (1861), p. 48. Boswell, Soame Jenyns, Lyttelton and Smollett.

168. Ibid., 3rd series, I, March 22 (1862), p. 232. Shebbeare, Smollett, and Lady Vane.

169. Ibid., 3rd series, VIII, November 11 (1865), p. 393. Smollett's characters.

170. Ibid., 5th series, I, May 16 (1874), p. 384. Smollett's letter to Richard Smith.

171. Ibid., 6th series, I, April 24 (1880), pp. 330-331. Smollett letter to Alexander Reid.

172. Ibid., 6th series, XI, June 20 (1885), p. 487. Smollett's medical degree.

173. Ibid., 6th series, XII, October 31, (1885), p. 349. Smollett's lodgings in Curzon street.

174. Ibid., 7th series, I, February 27 (1886), p. 178. Smollett's residences.

175. Ibid., 7th series, IV, December 24 (1887), p. 507. A projected edition of Smollett's works.

176. Ibid., 7th series, V, January 21 (1888), p. 58. Smollett's family; see #120, #121.

177. Ibid., 7th series, IX, May 24 (1890), p. 408. Death and burial of Smollett; see #87, #96, #131.

178. Ibid., 7th series, XII, September 12 (1891), p. 205. Smollett and Dibdin.

Ibid., 8th series, II, December 10 (1892), p. 466. 179.
Smollett and Goethe.

Ibid., 8th series, II, December 31 (1892), p. 533. 180.
Smollett and Goethe. See #179.

Ibid., 8th series, III, January 21 (1893), p. 55. 181.
Smollett and Goethe. See #179, #180.

Ibid., 8th series, IV, November 25 (1893), p. 426. 182.
Smollett's widow.

Ibid., 8th series, VIII, December 7, (1895), p. 441. 183.
Smollett's death; cf. #177.

Ibid., 9th series, I, March 12 (1898), pp. 201-202. 184.
Smollett's death and burial; cf. #177, #183.

Ibid., 9th series, I, April 16 (1898), pp. 309-311. 185.
Smollett's death and burial; cf. #177, #183, #184.

Ibid., 10th series, IX, February 1 (1908), p. 8. 186.
Spiritual Quixote and Smollett.

Ibid., 12th series, IX, July 16 (1921), p. 48. 187.
Smollett and Pope.

Ibid., 12th series, XII, October 11 (1924), pp. 403-404. 188.
Ascription of "A north Briton extraordinary" to Smollett.

Olive, M., The elements of caricature in Smollett's 189.
novels. Ms. thesis for diplôme d'études
supérieures, Univ. de Paris (Sorbonne), 1922.

Peach, R.E.M., Street lore of Bath, London, 190.
1893.
Some mention of Smollett.

[Perrin], W.G., "Tobias George Smollett," The 191.
mariner's mirror, X, January (1924), p. 94.

Pérrone, J.W., Über englische Zustande im 192.
XVIII. Jahrhundert nach den Romanen von
Fielding und Smollett, Berlin, 1890.

Smollett Criticism, 1770-1924. 29

Perry, T. S., English literature in the eighteenth 193.
    century, New York, 1883.
    Smollett on Gothic architecture, p. 144 n;
    see pp. 217, 351.

Poetzsche, Erich, Samuel Richardsons Belesenheit, 194.
    Kiel, 1908.
    See p. 80.

Portfolio, new series, VI (1811), pp. 412-431. 195.
    Smollett and Fielding.
    See #98, #99, #137.

Portfolio, series 5, XI (1821), pp. 134-135. 196.
    Washington Irving and Smollett. See #149.

The Practitioner, XXIII, January (1906), 197.
    pp. 109-115.
    "Some medical worthies of Bath."

Prowse, W. J., "Smollett at Nice," Macmillan's 198.
    magazine, XXI (1870), p. 527.
    See #16, #80, #97, #132.

Quarterly review, I (1809), p. 338. 199.
    Smollett's pictures of naval life.
    See #100, #129.

Ibid., XXXIV (1826), p. 376. 200.
    Smollett and Scott. See #35, #162.

Ibid., LIX (1837), p. 484. 201.
    Smollett and Dickens, See #81.

Ibid., LXIV (1839), p. 349. 202.
    Smollett and Dickens. See #81, #201.

Ibid., CIII (1858), pp. 66-108. 203.
    A review of the novels. Same article in
    Living age, LVI, pp. 641-695.

Ibid., CLXIII (1886), pp. 48-50. 204.
    Smollett and Fielding. See #98, #195.

Raleigh, Walter, The English novel, London, 1894. 205.
    See pp. 183-190.

Reeve, Clara, The progress of romance (Facsimile text Society, New York, 1930) London, 1785. See # 58, # 148. 206.

Rivington, Septimus, The publishing family of Rivington, London 1919.
Some mention of Smollett. 207.

Robinson, C. N., and Leyland, John, The British tar in fact and fiction, London, 1909. 208.

Roscoe, T., Miscellaneous works of Tobias Smollett, London, 1841.
A memoir by the editor. 209.

Saintsbury, George, Works of Tobias Smollett, London, 1895. 12v.
Critical introductions. 210.

_____, The English novel, London, 1913
See pp. 115-126. 211.

_____, The peace of the Augustans, London, 1916.
See p. 134. Roderick, Peregrine and Bramble. 212.

[Sargent, W.], "Some inedited memorials of Smollett," Atlantic Monthly, III, June (1859), pp. 693-703. 213.

Schneider, A., Die Entwicklung des seeromans in England im XVII. und XVIII. Jahrhunderts, Leipzig, 1901. 214.

Schudt, E., Das Ausland in Smolletts romanen, Giessen, 1923. 215.

Schyler, E., "Smollett in search of health," The Nation, XLVIII, (1889), pp. 423-425, 444-445. 216.

Scott, Walter, The novels of Tobias Smollett, to which is prefixed a memoir of the life of the author (Novelist's library, II, III), London, 1821. 2v. 217.

Smollett Criticism, 1770-1924.   31

Scots magazine, XXXIII (1771), p. 558.   218.
    Obituary notice.

Ibid., LVIII (1796), pp. 725-726.   219.
    Brief biographical notice.

Scotish review, XXIII (1894), p. 227.   220.
    "Prurient incidents in Smollett's career."

Seccombe, Thomas, "Smollett" in Dictionary of   221.
    national biography.
    See #15.

_____, "Smelfungus goes south," Cornhill   222.
    magazine, LXXXIV (1901), p. 192.

Smeaton, Oliphant, Tobias Smollett, Edinburgh,   223.
    1897.
    Popular life; undocumented.

Southern literary messenger, V (1839), p. 183 ff.   224.
    Unfavorable notices.

Ibid., VIII (1842), p. 354.   225.
    Unfavorable notices.

Stephen, Leslie, English thought in the eighteenth   226.
    century, London, 1876. 2v.
    See II, pp. 378, 380.

_____, Hours in a library, London, 1892.   227.
    3v.
    See II, p. 177.

Stephens, F. G., Catalogue of prints and drawings   228.
    in the British Museum, London, 1870.
    Vs. III, IV contain descriptions of many
    political cartoons in which Smollett figures.

Taine, H. A., Historie de la littérature anglaise,   229.
    Paris, 1863-64. 4v.
    See III, p. 319 ff. See #83, #119.

Thackeray, William, The English humourists of   230.
    the eighteenth century, 2nd. edition, London,
    1853.
    Hogarth, Fielding and Smollett, pp. 219-268.

231. Times literary supplement (London), 17 March, 1921.
"Tobias Smollett." An article celebrating the bicentenary of Smollett's birth.

232. Timperley, C. H., Encyclopaedia of literary and typographical anecdote, London, 1842.
Some general notices.

233. Tuckerman, Bayard, A history of English prose fiction from Sir Thomas Malory to George Eliot, New York, 1882.
See pp. 211-217.

234. Vigo, Pietro, Livorno, Bergamo, 1915.
A panorama of Monte Nero and references to Smollett's villa near Leghorn.

235. Watson, Harold F., The sailor in English fiction and drama, 1550-1800, New York, 1831.

236. Wershoven, F. J., Smollett et Lesage, Brieg, 1883.
Beilage zum Programm der Königlichen Ober-Realschule zu Brieg. Beyond Scott's criticism (see #217), perhaps, the best brief (13 pp.) critical notice.

237. Westminster magazine, III, (1775), p. 225 ff.
Extended commentary on the novels.

238. Ibid., IV (1776), pp. 129, 522.
Smollett and Richardson.
See #145, #194.

239. Westminster review, VII (1827), p. 343.
Doctrinal novels and Smollett.

240. Ibid., XX (1834), p. 153.
Some general criticism.

241. Ibid., XXVII (1837), p. 313.
Smollett and Dickens. See #81, #201, #202.

242. Wilson, David, Memorials of Edinburgh in the olden time, Edinburgh, 1872.
References to Smollett.

Smollett Criticism, 1770-1924. 33

243. ———, Reminiscences of old Edinburgh, Edinburgh, 1878. 2v.
   References to Smollett.

244. Wilson, F. W., Dickens in seinen Beziehungen zu den Humoristen Fielding und Smollett, Leipzig, 1899.

245. Wonderful prophecies: being a dissertation on the existence, nature, and extent of the prophetic powers in the human mind; and a remarkable prophecy of Dr. Smollett just before his death..., London, 1795.
   The most unusual Smollett item.

246. Yvon, Paul, La vie d'un dilettante, Paris, 1924.
   France in the works of Smollett.

247. Young, Arthur, Travels during the years 1787, 1788, 1789..., Dublin, 1793. 2v.
   See I, p. 398. Smollett and the climate of Nice.

III. Plays and Poems

248. Campbell, Thomas, Specimens of the British poets, London, 1819. 7v.
   See VI, 221.

249. Carey, Henry F., Lives of the English poets from Johnson to Kirke White, London, 1846.
   Notices of Smollett as a poet.
   See pp. 119-146.

250. Chalmers, Alexander, Works of the English poets, London, 1810. 21v.
   See XV, pp. 543, 551-553.

251. Gilfillan, George, The poetical works of Johnson, Parnell, Gray, and Smollett, Edinburgh, 1855.
   Memoir, critical dissertation, explanatory notes.

252. London review, V (1777), p. 206.
   A commentary on the plays and poems.

Monthly review, LVII (1777), p. 77.   253.
    A commentary on the plays and poems.

Westminster magazine, V (1777), p. 435.   254.
    A commentary on the plays and the poems.

IV. Translations

Fitzmaurice-Kelly, J., ed., The adventures of   255.
    Gil Blas of Santillane, (World's Classics),
    1907. 2v.
    Critical introduction.

Mayhew, A., "Smollett's translation of Gil Blas," 256.
    The Academy, XLII, October 8 (1892), p. 313.

Morton-Fullerton, Arthur, The adventures of Gil   257.
    Blas, London, 1913.
    Critical preface. The text is not Smollett's
    translation. It is that of Benjamin Heath
    Malkin (London, 1809, 4v.) Malkin's trans-
    lation is often issued as Smollett's. See
    George Saintsbury's edition of Malkin's trans-
    lation which he issued as that of Smollett
    (Edinburgh, 1881).

Tytler, A. F. (Lord Woodhouselee), Essay on the   258.
    principles of translation, London, 1791.
    Some notice of Smollett's translation of
    Don Quixote.

V. Historical Writings

Alison, Archibald, Essays political, historical,   259.
    and miscellaneous, London, 1850. 3v.
    See III, p. 322. Smollett as historian.

The Bee, or literary intelligencer, III (1791),   260.
    pp. 90-91.
    Smollett as historian.

Monthly magazine, XXII (1806), p. 443.   261.
    Smollett as an historian.

Notes and queries, 11th series, II, August 13   262.
    (1910), p. 129.
    Continuators of Smollett's History of England.

Ibid., 11th series, II, September 10 (1910),   263.
    p. 213.
    A further notice of #262.

Ibid., 11th series, II, September 24 (1910),   264.
    p. 256.
    A further notice of #262, #263.

Ibid., 11th series, II, November 12 (1910), p. 393.   265.
    A further notice of #262, #263, #264.

Trevelyan, G. O., Life and letters of Thomas   266.
    Babington Macaulay, New York, 1877. 2v.
    See II, p. 37. Macaulay's censures of
    Smollett as historian.

VI. History and Adventures of an Atom

Muhlberg, E., Tobias Smolletts History and ad-   267.
    ventures of an atom und Charles Johnstones
    Chrysal or the adventures of a guinea.
    Zwei polit. Satire. des 18 Jahrh. Ein
    beitrag zur Geschichte des engl. Satire.,
    Halle (ms. dissertation), 1924.
    See further #69.

VII. Travels through France and Italy

National review, LXXV (1920), pp. 344-353.   268.
    A general commentary.

Schuyler, Eugene, Italian influences, London, 1901.   269.
    See pp. 220-245.

Seccombe, Thomas, ed., Travels through France   270.
    and Italy, (World's Classics), 1907.
    See pp. v-lx. A critical introduction.
    See further #16, #23, #97, #132, #198,
    #216.

VIII. Adventures of Roderick Random

Gentleman's magazine, XLI (1771), p. 571.   271.
    Smollett's Hugh Strap.

Notes and queries, #68, February 15 (1851), p. 123.   272.
    Smollett's celebrated Hugh Strap.

Ibid., #175, March 5 (1853), p. 234. 273.
Hugh Strap.

Ibid., 7th series, V, February 18 (1888), p. 133. 274.
Hugh Strap.

Ibid., 7th series, VIII, November 2 (1889), p. 348. 275.
Hugh Strap.

Ibid., 7th series, VIII, November 9, (1889), p. 377. 276.
Hugh Strap.

Ibid., 7th series, VIII, December 14 (1889), p. 475. 277.
Hugh Strap.

Ibid., 8th series, II, December 10 (1892), p. 463. 278.
A general commentary.

Ibid., 8th series, III, January 7, (1893), p. 12. 279.
A general commentary.

Ibid., 9th series, XII, September 12 (1903), p. 205. 280.
Original of Squire Gawkie.

Ibid., 11th series, II, July 9 (1910), p. 26. 281.
Hugh Strap.

Townsend, G. H., ed., The adventures of Roderick 282.
Random, London, 1857.
A critical introduction.

See further #7, #26, #30, #38, #78, #100, #115,
#129, #138, #154, #157, #199, #208, #210,
#214, #235.

IX. Adventures of Peregrine Pickle

Huse, W. W. "Pickle and Pickwick," Washington 283.
university studies, X (1922), pp. 143-154.

Notes and queries, 11th series, II, November 26 284.
(1910), p. 421.
Original of Commodore Trunnion.

Scribner's Monthly, XIV (1877), p. 446. 285.
Verse criticism.

Smollett Criticism, 1770-1924.

See further #7, #26, #30, #38, #115, #138, #210.

X. Adventures of Ferdinand, Count Fathom

Critical review, LXIX (1790), p. 118. 286.
    Gothic elements.

Ibid., 2nd series, X (1794), p. 349. 287.
    Gothic elements.

Modern language notes, XVII (1902), p. 230. 288.
    Otway's Orphan and Smollett's Count Fathom.

See further #30, #78, #115, #138, #210.

XI. Adventures of Sir Launcelot Greaves

Büge, Karl, Untersuchungen über Smolletts Roman 289.
    Adventures of Sir Launcelot Greaves
    insbesondere über seine technik und seine
    Quellen, Köingsberg (ms. dissertation), 1921.
    Summary in Inaug. Diss. d. phil. Fak.
    Konigsberg L. P., 1921.

Dermody, Thomas, The Harp of Erin, London, 290.
    1807. 2v.
    Verse praise.

See further #30, #78, #115, #138, #210.

XII. The Expedition of Humphry Clinker

Court and city magazine, II (1771), p. 310. 291.
    A review and notice.

Critical review, XXXII (1771), pp. 81-88. 292.
    A review and notice.

Dobson, Austin, "The typography of Humphry 293.
    Clinker," in 18th century vignettes,
    series 2, London, 1894.

General magazine, IV (1790), pp. 397-398. 294.
    Matthew Bramble and Andrew Macdonald.

Hibernian magazine, I (1771), p. 324.   295.
    A review and notice.

Notes and queries, 3rd series, XI, May 4 (1867),   296.
    p. 353.
    Some problems.

Ibid., 3rd series, XI, June 15 (1867), p. 491.   297.
    Some problems.

Ibid., 8th series, VI, December (1894), pp. 486-   298.
    487.
    Some problems.

Ibid., 11th series, IV, October 28 (1911), p. 348.   299.
    Dr. Arnold on Humphry Clinker.

Perth magazine, I (1772), p. 5.   300.
    Matthew Bramble.

Town and country magazine, III (1771), pp. 317, 323.   301.
    A review and notice.

Westminster magazine, XIII (1785), p. 137.   302.
    Some observations.

Universal magazine of knowledge and pleasure,   303.
    XLIX (1771), pp. 256-257.
    Some critical remarks and review.
    See further #7, #26, #30, #56, #78, #89,
    #115, #120, #138.

The Percy anecdotes, 40 parts, compiled by   304.
    Sholto and Reuben Percy (Joseph Clinton
    Robertson and Thomas Byerley), London,
    1820-23.
    Some mention of Smollett.

Westminster review, CLXXVI, April (1868), p. 144.   305.
    Smollett's translation of Don Quixote.

II.

Smollett Criticism, 1925-1945:
a Compilation.

Copyright 1947 by Francesco Cordasco

Preface

This opusculo is a labor of love. So much advance has, in the last generation, been made in Smollett scholarship, that for the Smollett enthusiast this is truly the Annus Mirabilis. In the next few years most of the Smollett problems will have been resolved, and a full portraiture of the versatile and prolific genius of Smollett will have been achieved. Although this compilation limits itself to the years 1925-1945, there is no arbitrariness in the chronology. The year 1925 seems to the author the important year of an earnest effort, with modern bibliographic and research methods, to approach the maze of Smollett problems. The year 1945 is arbitrary, but its choice is judicious, in the light of its immediacy. However, the important dissertation of Fred Boege, Smollett's Reputation as a Novelist (Princeton University Press, 1947) must be mentioned. Dr. Boege has chosen to deal with Smollett's English and American reputation, and although he has not achieved the felicity and definitiveness of the Joliat companion work, still he has assembled an important amount of information.

Thanks are due Nathan Resnick, Elliott Gatner and James Foster, colleagues and friends, for helpful suggestion.

F. C.

Carmela Madorma Cordasco

Matri Meae
Cujus nomen vivae
Huic opusculo praetexi Debuerat
Quod materno amore inceptum fovebat
mortuae peractum
Amantissimus Dedico

List of Abbreviation Used

PQ	Philological Quarterly
MLN	Modern Language Notes
TLS	(London) Times Literary Supplement
PMLA	Publications of the Modern Language Association of America
RLC	Revue de la Littérature Comparée
JEGP	Journal of English and Germanic Philology
RES	Review of English Studies
N&Q	Notes & Queries
MP	Modern Philology
EA	Études Anglaises
SP	Studies in Philology

Smollett Criticism, 1925-1945: a Compilation.

      The year 1925 is important in the study of Smollett. In that year Howard S. Buck published his Study in Smollett, chiefly "Peregrine Pickle" (Yale University Press), and with it inaugurated a new era in Smollett scholarship. Primarily, his study showed how inadequate and limited the criticism of Smollett had been, and it helped arouse the careful attention which, since 1925, has been focused on the novelist without interruption. The following compilation, exhaustive, and chronological in arrangement, will demonstrate the direction the new study of Smollett has taken.

1925

1. Howard S. Buck, A Study in Smollett, chiefly Peregrine Pickle, with a complete collation of the first and second editions. New Haven, Yale University Press.
   Cf. PQ, V (1926), 369.

2. Cecil K. Drinker, "Doctor Smollett," Annals of Medical History, VII, (March), 31-47. Bibliography, 46-47.

1926

3. Lewis Melville, The Life and Letters of Tobias Smollett. London.

4. Edward S. Noyes, The Letters of Tobias Smollett. Harvard University Press.
   Discovery of 15 hitherto unprinted letters; new material to 13 letters already published.

5. _____, "A note on Peregrine Pickle and Pygmalion," MLN, XLI, 327-30.

1927

6. Howard S. Buck, Smollett as a Poet. New Haven, Yale University Press.

Edward S. Noyes, "Another Smollett Letter," 7.
MLN, XLII, 231-35.

Harold Stein, "Smollett's Imprisonment," TLS, 8.
May 5, 318.
Fixes the exact dates.

1928

Howard S. Buck, "A Roderick Random play, 9.
1748," MLN, XLIII, 111-12.

Allan D. McKillop, "Notes on Smollett," PQ, 10.
VII, 368-74.

1929

Lee M. Ellison, "Elizabethan Drama and the works 11.
of Smollett," PMLA, XLIV, 842-62.

Lewis M. Knapp, "The Classical element in 12.
Smollett's Roderick Random," Classical
Weekly, XXIII, 9-15, 17-19.

1930

Lewis M. Knapp, "Ann Smollett, wife of Tobias 13.
Smollett," PMLA, XLV, 1035-49.

Allan D. McKillop, "Smollett's first Comedy," 14.
MLN, XLV, 396-97.

1931

A. C. Hunter, "Les Livres de Smollett détenus 15.
par la douane à Boulogne en 1763," RLC,
XI, 736-37.

Lewis M. Knapp, "A rare Satire on Smollett," 16.
TLS, Oct. 8, 778.

_____, "Smollett's verses and their musical 17.
settings in the 18th century," MLN, XLVI,
224-32.

Smollett Criticism, 1925-1945.   47

1932

Howard S. Buck, "A new Smollett anecdote,"   18.
  MLN, XLVII, 90-91.

————, "Smollett and Akenside," JEGP,   19.
  XXXI, 10-26.

Lewis M. Knapp, "A sequel to Smollett's Humphry   20.
  Clinker," TLS, Oct. 6, 716.

————, "Elizabeth Smollett, daughter of   21.
  Tobias Smollett," RES, VIII, 312-15.

————, "Smollett and Le Sage's The Devil   22.
  upon Krutches," MLN, XLVII, 91-93.

————, "Smollett's early years in London,"   23.
  JEGP, XXXI, 220-27.

————, "Smollett's works as printed by Wm.   24.
  Strahan, with an unpublished letter of
  Smollett to Strahan," Library, 4th series,
  XIII, 282-91.

A. Lawrence, "L'influence de Lesage sur   25.
  Smollett," RLC, XII, 533-45.

J. M. Purcell, "A note on Smollett's language,"   26.
  MLN, XLVII, 93-94.

1933

J. H. Birss, "A Letter to Tobias Smollett,"   27.
  N&Q, CLXIV, 315-16.

————, "Note on Smollett letter #37," N&Q,   28.
  CLXV, 189.

Lewis M. Knapp, "More Smollett letters," MLN,   29.
  XLVIII, 246-49.

Coleman O. Parsons, "Smollett's influence on   30.
  The Rivals," N&Q, CLXIV, 39-41.

1934

J. H. Birss, "A letter of Tobias G. Smollett," 31.
N&Q, CLXVI, 189.

Lewis M. Knapp, "The naval scenes in Roderick 32.
Random," PMLA, XLIX, 593-98.
The historical accuracy of the naval scenes.

1935

Tobias Smollett, An Essay on the External use of 33.
water. Edited by Claude E. Jones, Baltimore,
The Johns Hopkins University Press. (pp. 31-
82: reprinted from the Bulletin of the Institute
of the History of Medicine.
Smollett as a therapeutist.

A. J. Grant, "Smollett and billiards," TLS, 34.
Nov. 16, 746.

Eugène Joliat, Smollett et la France. Paris. 35.
(Bibliothèque de la Revue de littérature
comparée)
A detailed commentary of Smollett's French
sources, his travel and residence in France,
and his influence in France, with an appended
bibliography of European translations of
Smollett's works (pp. 255-69).

Claude Jones, "A Smollett letter," MLN, L, 36.
242-43.

George M. Kahrl, "The influence of Shakespeare 37.
on Smollett" in Essays in Dramatic Literature: the Parrott presentation volume,
pp. 399-420. Princeton University Press.

Lewis M. Knapp, "Smollett and the case of James 38.
Annesley," TLS, Dec. 28, 899.

1936

Montgomery Carmichael, "Tobias Smollett a 39.
Livorno," Liburnicivitas, IX, 114-123.
Smollett's residence at Leghorn. Cf. P. Vigo,
Livorno. Bergamo, 1915.

Lewis M. Knapp, "An important Smollett letter," 40.
RES, XII, 75-77.

L. F. Powell, "William Huggins and Tobias 41.
Smollett," MP, XXXIV, 179-92.

1937

Samuel H. Brown, "Tobias Smollett, physician," 42.
University of Pennsylvania General Magazine
and Historical Chronicle, XXXIX, 252-55.

W. Roberts, "Gainsborough and Smollett," TLS, 43.
Sept. 18, 675. Cf. ibid. by Roberts, Sept.
25, 695; by L. Rice-Oxley, ibid. Oct. 2,
715; by M. H. Grant, ibid. Oct. 9, 735;
by L. F. Powell, ibid. Oct. 16, 759.
On the identification of a landscape painter
in Humphry Clinker.

1938

Eugene Joliat, "Millin's use of Smollett's 44.
Travels," RLC, XVIII, 510-14.

George M. Kahrl, "Travel and the prose fiction of 45.
Tobias Smollett," Harvard University Summaries of Theses, 330-33.

L. M. Price, "Smollett, Junger, und Stephanie 46.
der Jungere," Monatschrift für deutschen
Unterricht, XXX, 157-62.

J. M. Purcell, "Smollett on oats as food for 47.
Scots," PMLA, LIII, 629.

1939

Jean Bélanger, "Note sur Roderick Random et 48.
l'expédition de Carthagène," EA, III, 250-51.

Eugène Joliat, "Smollett, editor of Voltaire," MLN, 49.
LIV, 429-36.

W. D. Taylor, "Tobias Smollett, M. D., Aberdeen, 50.
1750," Aberdeen University Review, XXVI,
125-35.

1940

Henry R. Viets, "Smollett, the War of Jenkin's ear, and an account of the expedition to Carthagena, 1743," De Libris, Feb. 28, 226-33. 51.

H. P. Vincent, "Tobias Smollett's assault on Gordon and Groom," RES, XVI, 183-88. 52.

1941

George M. Kahrl, "Captain Robert Stobo," Virginia Magazine of History and Biography, XLX, 141-51; 254-68.
Stobo was an acquaintance of Smollett; he may have been the model for Lieutenant Lismahago in Humphry Clinker. 53.

Louis L. Martz, "Smollett and the expedition of Carthagena," PMLA, LVI, 428-46. 54.

L. F. Norwood, "The authenticity of Smollett's Ode to Independence," RES, XVII, 55-64. 55.

1942

James R. Foster, "Smollett's pamphleteering foe Shebbeare," PMLA, LVII, 1053-1100. 56.

Claude Jones, Smollett Studies (University of California publications in English, IX, #2)
 I. Smollett and the Navy
 II. Smollett and the Critical Review
 III. Appendixes: Knowles; opponents to the Critical; two letters.
 Bibliography, 129-133
 Cf. PQ XXII, 173; XXIII, 177 57.

Louis L. Martz, The Later Career of Tobias Smollett (Yale Studies in English, XCVII), Yale University Press.
Cf. PQ, XXII, 174 58.

Alice Parker, "Tobias Smollett and the Law," SP, XXXIX, 354-58. 59.

Smollett's encounters with the law and
the light thrown on his character and the
novels.

V. S. Pritchett, "Books in General," New States- 60.
man and Nation, XXIII, 145.
A brief commentary on the novels.

1943

Francesco Cordasco, Smollett en España. Madrid 61.
Translations; history of reputation;
bibliography.

Lewis M. Knapp, "Smollett's friend Smith," TLS, 62.
Oct. 9, 492.

Henry W. Meikle, "New Smollett Letters," TLS, 63.
July 24, 360; ibid. July 31, 372.
The text of seven letters to Dr. Carlyle.

1944

Francesco Cordasco, Ensayo sobre las obras de 64.
Smollett y la Gil Blas de Lesage.
Salamanca.

Lewis M. Knapp, "Rex versus Smollett: more 65.
data on the Smollett - Knowles libel case,"
MP, 221-27.

———, "Smollett's letter to Philip Miller," 66.
TLS, June 24, 312.

———, "Smollett and the elder Pitt," MLN, 67.
LIX, 250-57.
Smollett's attitude toward Pitt. Criticism
in the Gazetteer and London Daily Advertiser
in 1762.

1945

George M. Kahrl, Tobias Smollett: traveler - 68.
novelist. University of Chicago Press.
Cf. South Atlantic Quarterly, XLIV, 452-53;
MLN, LX, 499-500; TLS, June 30, 309; N&Q,
CLXXXIX, 22.

Lewis M. Knapp, "Smollett and Garrick," in   69.
    Elizabethan studies and other essays in
    honor of George F. Reynolds. (University
    of Colorado studies... in the Humanities,
    II, #4), 233-43.

Rufus Putney, "The Plan of Peregrine Pickle,"   70.
    PMLA, LX, 1051-65.

    Essentially, with the impetus furnished by Buck (#1), Smollett scholarship has, in the last twenty years, concerned itself with problems of biography, influence, and limitedly, with bibliography. The collection of letters by Noyes (#4) has proved invaluable in the elucidation of biographical data and has resulted in the subsequent letter discoveries (#7, 27, 29, 31, 36, 40, 57, 63, 66). Stein (#8) and Foster (#56) have fixed the dates of Smollett's imprisonment; and Martz (#54) has, once and for all, established Smollett's role in the ill-fated expedition to Carthegena. Knapp has distinguished himself in the elucidation of important biographical detail (#13, 21, 23, 32, 38, 61, 65, 67, 69). Joliat has importantly dealt with Smollett's reputation in France and the French influences (#35). However, much still remains to be done.

    There is an immediate need for a Smollett biography which utilizes the important discoveries made. Professor Knapp has announced one (see The Johnsonian News Letter, VI, #3, 8: July, 1946), but, as yet, it has not appeared. A great need exists for an exhaustive Smollett bibliography. Miss Norwood is said to have one in preparation (see CBEL, II, 523), but it, too, has not yet appeared. Virtually no work has been done with the historical works of Smollett. Excepting the work of Joliat (#35, 49), no effort has been made to evaluate the translations of Smollett of the Don Quixote and the Gil Blas. All in all, we are the threshold of the appearance of the major works in Smollett scholarship.

Addenda

1925

Arnold Whitridge, Tobias Smollett: a study of   71.
    his miscellaneous works. Brooklyn, N.Y.
    A Vorarbeit for an extended critical biography.

1935

Lewis M. Knapp, "The Publication of Smollett's 72.
  Complete History...and Continuation,"
  Library, 4th Series, XVI, 295-308.

1941

Louis L. Martz, "Tobias Smollett and the Universal 73.
  History," MLN LVI, 1-12.
  Smollett's contribution: some 3000 folio pages.

III.

Samuel Richardson
a List of Critical Studies
Published from 1896 to 1946

Copyright 1948 by Francesco Cordasco

Preface

There is no complete bibliography of Richardson. The work of Sale (# 9) does not collect criticism, and although, as a descriptive and ennumerative bibliography of the works, it is excellent, it is to be regretted that Professor Sale did not go on to a critical bibliography. For criticism, the student must turn to the general work of Tobin (# 10), the list of Downs (# 7) or the appendices of McKillop (# 54) and Dottin (# 29) in their excellent biographic studies. The following list is to serve as a guide to the criticism of Richardson in the last half century, a period particularly rich in the new appreciation of Richardson's importance and wide influence. Particularly refreshing is the rejection of the sterile German dissertation criticism (# 20, # 70, # 81) which assigned to Marivaux's Vie de Marianne great influence on Pamela. Although the French critics have continued in this absurd (and chronologically impossible) contention (# 37), the works of Crane (# 120, # 121) and Thompson (# 86) have assigned it to its proper place. Even M. Van Tieghem (# 92) seems convinced. The publication of George Cheyne's letters to Richardson (# 55) helps answer some questions and makes more eventful a seemingly uneventful life.

In the compilation most of the titles are sufficiently clear as to the nature of the criticism; where this is not so, some brief annotation has been given. Important reviews have also been cited, and some cross-reference made to criticism in agreement or disagreement with particular entries.

Professor James R. Foster, whose Pre-Romantic novel in England will undoubtedly add much to the appreciation of Richardson, has made some suggestions for the list.

F. C.

Contents

I.	Bibliography.	61
II.	Biography and General Criticism	62
III.	The Letters	69
IV.	Pamela.	69
V.	Clarissa	70
VI.	Sir Charles Grandison	70
VII.	Foreign Reputation and Influences.	71

Abbreviations

ES	Englische Studien
HLQ	Huntington Library Quarterly
HTB	Herald Tribune Book Supplement
JEGP	Journal of English and Germanic Philology
LM	London Mercury
MLN	Modern Language Notes
MLR	Modern Language Review
MP	Modern Philology
N&Q	Notes and Queries
PMLA	Publications of Modern Language Association
PQ	Philological Quarterly
RAA	Revue Anglo-américaine
RELV	Revue de l'Enseignement des Langues vivantes
RES	Review of English Studies
RLC	Revue de la litterature comparêe
TBR	New York Times Book Review
TLS	London Times Literary Supplement

Samuel Richardson: a List of Critical Studies,
Published from 1896-1946.

I. Bibliography

1. Bartholomew, A. T., "Samuel Richardson," in Cambridge history of English literature, New York, 1913, X, pp. 465-467.

2. Block, Andrew, The English novel, 1740-1850. A short catalogue..., London, 1939.

3. Dottin, Paul, "Du nouveau sur Richardson (documents inédits)," RAA, V (1928), 557-61. See PQ VIII (April 1929), 199.

4. ———, "Du nouveau sur Richardson (documents inédits)," RAA, VI (1929), 258-61.

5. ———, "Du nouveau sur Richardson (documents inédits)," RAA, VII (1929), 55-59.

6. ———, "Du nouveau sur Richardson (documents inédits)," RAA, VII (1930), 432-34. An unpublished letter of October 9, 1750.

7. Downs, B. W., "Samuel Richardson," in Cambridge bibliography of English literature, New York, 1941, II, pp. 514-17.

8. McKillop, Alan D., "Samuel Richardson's advise to an apprentice," JEGP, XLII (1943), 40-54. The authorship of The apprentice's vade mecum (1733).

9. Sale, William M., Samuel Richardson, a bibliographical record of his literary career with historical notes, New Haven, Yale University Press, 1936.

Tobin, James E., Eighteen century literature and 10.
its cultural background: a bibliography, New
York, Fordham University Press, 1939,
pp. 149-150.
See also # 14, # 21, # 23, # 29, # 42, # 54,
55, # 69, # 86, # 94, # 99, # 108, # 112,
114, # 115, # 118, # 119.

II. Biography and General Criticism

Addleshaw, S., "A pioneer - Samuel Richardson," 11.
Church quarterly review, CX (1930), 297-315.

Anonymous, Samuel Richardson: his writings and 12.
his friends, New York, 1901.

Askew, H., "Samuel Richardson's birthplace," 13.
N&Q, CLXIX (1935), 263.
See reply by F. Williamson, Ibid., 300-301.

Baker, Ernest A., The history of the English 14.
novel: intellectual realism from Richardson
to Sterne, London, 1930.

Baldwin, C. E., "Marivaux's place in the develop- 15.
ment of character portrayal," PMLA, XXVII
(1912), 168-187.

Binz-Winiger, E., Erziehungsfragen in den 16.
Romanen von Richardson, Fielding, Smollett,
Goldsmith und Sterne, Zurich, 1924.

Birkhead, E., "Sentiment and Sensibility in the 17.
18th century novel," Essays and studies,
XI (1925).

Birrell, A., Res judicatae, New York, 1908. 18.

Boas, F. S., From Richardson to Pinero: some 19.
innovators and idealists, London, 1936.

Broadus, E. K., "Mr. Richardson arrives," LM, 20.
XXVIII (1933), 425-35.

Brown, Herbert R., "Richardson and Sterne in 21.
the Massachusetts magazine," New England
magazine, V (1932), 65-82.

Samuel Richardson

Collins, Baker, "Joseph Highmore, Samuel   22.
   Richardson, and Lady Bradshaigh," HLQ,
   VII (1944), 316-20.

Cordasco, F., "La fortuna di Samuel Richardson   23.
   in Italia," Rivista universitaria, I (1943),
   37-58.

Danielowski, Emma, Richardsons erster roman,   24.
   Berlin, 1917.

_____, Die journale der frühen Quäker,   25.
   Berlin, 1926.

Dibelius, Wilhelm, Englische romankunst. Die   26.
   technik des englischen romans in achtzehnten
   und zu anfang des neunzehnten Jahrhunderts,
   Berlin, 1910.

Dobson, Austin, Richardson (English Men of   27.
   Letters Series), London, 1902.

Dottin, Paul, "Richardson," RELV, XLVI (1929)   28.
   164-67.
   A review of #31.

_____, Samuel Richardson, 1689-1761,   29.
   imprimeur de Londres, auteur de Pamela,
   Clarissa, et Grandison, Paris, 1931.
   Rev. by L. Cazamian, RH, CLXVIII (1931),
   395-97; J. W. Draper, PQ, X (1931), 320;
   J. A. Falconer, English Studies, XIV (1932),
   37-40: E. Legouis, RAA, IX (1931), 151-52;
   A. McKillop, MLN, XLVII (1932), 120-22;
   TLS, July 16, 1931, p. 561.

_____, "Samuel Richardson et le roman   30.
   épistolaire," RAA, XIII (1936), 481-99.

Downs, Brian W., Richardson, London, 1928.   31.
   Rev. TLS, January 31, 1929, p. 77; PQ,
   VIII (1929), 199; see #28.

Ewald, Eugen, Abbild und wunschbild der   32.
   gesellschaft bei Richardson und Fielding,
   Cologne, 1935.

33. Fischer, Walther, "Ein unbekannter brief David Garricks an Samuel Richardson," *Anglia*, LXIII (1939), 436-44.

34. Furman, H. B., "Richardson, Fielding, and the Andrews family," *Fortnightly review*, LXXVI (1901), 949-959.

35. Graham, H. G., *Literary and historical essays*, London, 1928.

36. Green, Frederick C., *Minuet - a critical survey of French and English literary ideas in the 18th century*, London, 1935.

37. Grimm, C., "Encore une fois la question Marivaux - Richardson," *RLC*, IV (1924).

38. Gwynn, Stephen, "Samuel Richardson," *Quarterly review*, CCLIX (1932), 315-30.

39. Hudson, W. H., *A quiet corner in a library*, London, 1915.

40. Huffman, C. H., *The 18th century novel in theory and practise*, Dayton, (1920).

41. Hughes, H. S., "Translations of the *Vie de Marianne* and their relation to contemporary English fiction," *MP*, XIV (1917).

42. _____, "A letter to Richardson from Edward Young," *MLN*, XXXVII (1922), 314-16.

43. Jackson, Holbrook, *Great English novelists*, London, 1908.

44. Kaye-Smith, Shelia, *Samuel Richardson*, London, 1911.

45. Krutch, Joseph W., "Samuel Richardson" in *Five masters: a study in the mutations of the novel*, New York, 1930.

46. Lefever, Charlotte, "Richardson's paradoxical success," *PMLA*, XLVIII (1933), 856-60.

47. Levy, L., Einfluss der moralischen wochenschriften auf Richardsons romane, Köingsberg, 1921.

48. Macaulay, G. C., "Richardson and his French predecessors," MLR, VIII (1913).
See further #17, #30, #79, #92, #96.

49. Martin, Burns, "Richardson's removal to Salisbury Court," MLN, XLV (1930), 469.

50. McCullough, Bruce, "Samuel Richardson" in Representative English novelists: Defoe to Conrad, New York, 1946.

51. McKillop, Alan D., "Richardson, Young and the Conjectures," MP, XXII (1925)

52. ———, "The personal relations between Fielding and Richardson," MP, XXVIII (1931), 423-33.

53. ———, "Richardson's early years as a printer," RES, IX (1933), 67-70.

54. ———, Samuel Richardson, printer and novelist, Chapel Hill, University of North Carolina Press, 1936.
Rev. TLS, April 10, p. 270; F. T. Wood, ES, LXXII, 115-17; C. G. Stillman, HTB, January 10, p. 17; J. W. Beach, JEGP, XXXVI, 438-40; G. Kitchin, MLR, XXXIII (1938), 27-29; H. Williams, RES, XIV (1938), 106-107; L. Kronenberger, TBR, December 27, p. 5.

55. Mullett, Charles F., ed., The letters of Doctor George Cheyne to Samuel Richardson (1733-1743), Columbia: University of Missouri Press, 1943.
Rev. Richard H. Shryock, AHR, XLIX, 279; PQ, XXIII (1944), 174-176.

56. Nairn, J. A., "Samuel Richardson and the Merchant Taylor's school," N&Q, CXLIX (1925), 421.

Noress, H., La vie de Marianne von Marivaux   57.
    und Richardsons Pamela, Marburg, 1920.

Notes and queries, 9th series, VIII, 163, 271.   58.
    Date of Richardson's birth.

Ibid., 9th series, XI, 349.   59.
    Richardson's use of the word "owl-light."

Ibid., 10th series, IX, 361, 503.   60.
    Richardson's kinfolk at Derby.

Ibid., 10th series, IX, 510; X, 96.   61.
    Richardson's family connexions.

Ibid., 11th series, III, 5.   62.
    Richardson and the English philosophers.

Ibid., 11th series, III, 123.   63.
    Richardson's family connexions in Derbyshire.

Ibid., 11th series, III, 124.   64.
    Richardson's references to the Methodists.

Ibid., 11th series, III, 127.   65.
    Richardson's birth.

Ibid., 11th series, XII, 320.   66.
    Richardson's birthplace. See # 58, # 65.

Ibid., 12th series, XI, 181, 224, 263, 303, 342,   67.
    383, 425, 465, 506.
    Richardson and his family circle.

Ibid., 12th series, XII, 6, 44, 56, 83, 126, 167,   68.
    209, 247, 287, 329, 366, 410, 446, 469, 504.
    Richardson and his family circle.

Pettit, Henry, "The text of Edward Young's letters   69.
    to Samuel Richardson," MLN, LVII (1942),
    668-70.
    On the imperfections of the text in the
    collected editions of Young.

Poetzsche, E., Samuel Richardsons Belesenheit,   70.
    Kiel, 1908.

Prinsen, J., De Roman in de 18e Eeuw in 71.
   West-Europa, Groningen, 1925.

Reade, A. L., "Samuel Richardson and Christ's 72.
   Hospital," TLS, February 5, 1931, p. 99.
   See comment by O. H. T. Dudley in TLS,
   February 17, p. 116.

Ronte, Heinz, Richardson und Fielding, Leipzig, 73.
   1935.
   See also # 16, # 34, # 52.

Sale, William M., "Samuel Richardson and Sir 74.
   William Harrington," TLS, August 29,
   1935, p. 537.

_____, "Samuel Richardson's house at 75.
   Fulham," N&Q, CLXIX (1935), 133-34.

Senex, ____: "Richardson and philology," N&Q, 76.
   CLXXXII (1942), 120.
   Ridicules Richardson for lack of philological
   knowledge in a passage in Pamela.

Schleck, Florian J., "Richardson on the Index," 77.
   TLS, April 25, 1935. p. 272.

Schlichting, H., Frauengestalten bei Samuel 78.
   Richardson, Freiburg, 1927.

Schmidt, E., Richardson, Rousseau und Goethe, 79.
   Jena, 1924 (1875).

Schucking, L. L., "Die Grundlagen des Richardson's- 80.
   chen Romans," Germanisch-romanische
   monatsschrift, XII (1924).

Schroers, C., "Ist Richardsons Pamela von 81.
   Marivauxs Vie de Marianne beeinflusst?"
   Englische studien, XLIV (1916).

Singer, G. F., The epistolary novel: its origin, 82.
   development, decline, and residuary influence,
   Philadelphia, 1933.

Swann, G. R., Philosophical parallelisms in six 83.
   English novelists, Philadelphia, 1929.

Taupin, René, "Richardson, Diderot, et l'art de conter," French Review, XII (1939), 181-94.   84.

Teubern, H. E. von, Edward Youngs gedanken über die originalwerke in einem schreiben an Samuel Richardson, Bohn, 1910.   85.

Thompson, C. L., Samuel Richardson: a biographical and critical study, London, 1900.   86.
Contains a list of plays in English, French, German, and Italian founded on Richardson's novels.

Thomsen, Ejner, Studier i Richardson's romaner, Kobenhavn, 1928.   87.

Thorne, W. B., "A famous printer: Samuel Richardson," Library, II (1901).   88.

Uhrstrom, W. P., Studies on the language of Samuel Richardson, Upsala, 1907.   89.

Utter, R. P., "On the alleged tediousness of Defoe and Richardson," University of California Chronicle, XXV (1923), 185-193.   90.

_____, and Needham, G. B., Pamela's daughters, New York, 1937.   91.

Van Tieghem, Paul, "Le roman sentimental en Europe de Richardson à Rousseau (1740-1761)," RLC, XX (1940), 129-51.   92.

Vreeland, W. U. D., Étude sur les rapports littéraires entre Genève et l'Angleterre jusqu'à la publication de la Nouvelle Héloise, Geneva, 1901.   93.

Wagenknecht, Edward, Cavalcade of the English novel, New York, 1943.   94.

Watters, Reginald E., "The vogue and influence of Samuel Richardson in America: a study of cultural conventions, 1742-1825. University of Wisconsin summaries of doctoral dissertations...for July, 1940-June, 1941, VI (1942), 295-97.   95.

Samuel Richardson

Wells, B. W., "Richardson and Rousseau," MLN, II (1896), 449-463. 96.
See also #79.

White, William, "Richardson: idealist or realist," MLR, XXXIV (1939), 240-41. 97.

Williams, I. A., "Two kinds of Richardsons," LM, VII (1923). 98.

III. The Letters

Downs, Brian W., ed., Familiar letters on important occasions by Samuel Richardson, London, 1928. 99.

Hornbeak, Katherine G., The complete letter writer in English, 1568-1800, Northhampton (Mass.), 1934. 100.

———, "Richardson's Familiar Letters and the domestic conduct books," Smith College studies in modern languages, XIX, ii (1938), 1-50. 101.
See also #47.

IV. Pamela

Beckstein, J., Richardsons Pamela nach ihrem Gedankengehalt betrachtet. Mit einem anhang: die Quellenfrage bei der Pamela, Bremen, 1929. 102.

Beckwith, F., "The anti-Pamelas," TLS, February 19, 1931, p. 135. 103.

Black, Frank G., "The continuations of Pamela," RAA, XIII (1936), 499-507. 104.

Dottin, Paul, "Les continuations de Pamela," RELV, XLVII (1930), 444-61. 105.

———, "L'accueil fait à Pamela," RAA, VII (1930), 505-19. 106.
See PQ, X (April, 1931), 207.

Miller, George M., "Newberry's edition of 107.
    Pamela," TLS, March 6, 1930, p. 196.

———, "The publisher of Pamela," TLS, 108.
    July 31, 1930, p. 628.
    See comment by C. J. Longman, Ibid.,
    August 28, 1930, p. 684.

Notes and queries, 9th series, XII, 141, 330. 109.
    General commentary.

Ibid., 10th series, IX, 361, 503. 110.
    Original of Pamela

Sale, William M., "The first dramatic version of 111.
    Pamela," Yale library gazette, IX (1935),
    83-88.
    See also #14, #15, #17, #26, #27, #29,
    #37, #40, #44, #54, #57, #81, #91, #94.

V. Clarissa

Eaves, T. C. Duncan, "The Harlowe family by 112.
    Joseph Highmore: a note on the illustration
    of Richardson's Clarissa," Huntington library
    quarterly, VII (1943), 89-96.
    Reproduces the painting.

Notes and queries, 11th series, VII, 250. 113.
    The first edition of Clarissa.

Sale, William M., "A bibliographical note on 114.
    Richardson's Clarissa," Library, XVI
    (1936), 448-51.

Ward, H. G., "Richardson's character of 115.
    Lovelace," MLR, VII (1912).
    See also #14, #15, #17, #26, #27, #29,
    #37, #40, #44, #54, #87, #91, #94.

VI. Sir Charles Grandison

Notes and queries, 11th series, III, 164. 116.
    Anne Howe and Charlotte Grandison.

Sale, William M., "Sir Charles Grandison and   117.
    the Dublin pirates," Yale university gazette,
    VII (1933), 80-86.
    See also #14, #15, #17, #26, #27, #29,
    #37, #40, #44, #54, #87, #91, #94.

VII. Foreign Reputation and Influences

Coe, Ada M., "Richardson in Spain," Hispanic   118.
    review. III (1935), 56-63.

Crane, R. S., "A note on Richardson's relations 119.
    to French fiction," MP, XVI (1919).

_____, "Richardson, Warburton and French   120.
    fiction," MLR, XVII (1922).

Donner, J. O. E., "Richardson in der deutschen   121.
    Romantik," Zeitschrift für vergleichende
    literaturgeschichte, X (1896).

Facteau, B. A., Les romans de Richardson sur   122.
    la scène française, Paris, (1927).

Ghijsen, H. C. M., "Wolff en Deken's romans   123.
    uit haar bloeitijd," De Gids, LXXXVII
    (April and May, 1923), 114-39; 241-64.
    Two Dutch women novelists of the 18th
    century in their relation to Richardson.

Liljegren, S. B., The English sources of   124.
    Goethe's Gretchen tragedy. A study on
    the life and taste of literary motives,
    Lund, 1937.

Notes and queries, 12th series, III, 7.   125.
    Richardson and Sterne on the Continent.

Price, Laurence M., "Richardson in the moral   126.
    weeklies of Germany," University of Wis-
    consin studies in language and literature,
    #22 (1925), pp. 169-83.
    See also #47.

_____, "On the reception of Richardson in   127.
    Germany," JEGP, XXV (1926), 7-33.

_____, "Richardson, Wetzlar and Goethe" 128.
in Mélanges offerts à Fernand Baldensperger,
II, Paris, 1930.

Purdie, E., "Some adventures of Pamela on the 129.
Continental stage," German studies presented
to H. G. Fiedler, Oxford University press,
1938, pp. 352-84.

Wilcox, Frank W., "Prévost's translation of 130.
Richardson's novels," University of California publications in modern philology,
XII (1927), 341-411.
Rev. George Ascoli, RC, LXI (1927),
455-56; MLR, XXIII (1928), 114-115; PQ,
VII (1928), 183.
See also #23, #37, #41, #47, #57, #81, #84,
#92, #96, #105, #106, #107.

IV.

Laurence Sterne
a List of Critical Studies
Published from 1896 to 1946

Copyright 1948 by Francesco Cordasco

Preface

This compilation like its predecessors has a twofold purpose: 1) to make immediately available recent criticism which will 2) enable the academician and antiquarian to turn his attention to those problems whose investigation has either been neglected or, perhaps, just begun. The criticism for Sterne relects the emphasis of the last fifty years. Concern with <u>Tristram Shandy</u> has been paramount, and, rightly, but the <u>Sermons</u> have received but passing attention, and, certainly, an extended study of the work <u>pro ecclesia dei</u> might prove elucidating and important. The <u>Letters</u> have provoked much discussion and it is to be regretted that the problems have not been resolved. The foreign reputation and influence of Sterne, so exhaustively noted in the German dissertations, have had a peculiar history. The Germans have remained only titles, and their neglect has led later historians to make much duplication.

One or two words about the list may be in order. Annotation has been kept at a minimum, and only important reviews have been noted. An alphabetical arrangement has been preferred, and the entries have purposely excluded the publisher name. The entry serves one purpose: sufficient information with which to locate the material. That, we feel, has been accomplished. Dr. Tristram Walker Metcalfe has given encouragement and made helpful suggestion.

F. C.

Contents

I.	Bibliography	79
II.	Biography and General Criticism	79
III.	Life and Opinions of Tristram Shandy, Gent.	86
IV.	A Sentimental Journey Through France and Italy	88
V.	The Letters	89
VI.	Foreign Influence and Reputation	90
VII.	Miscellaneous	91
VIII.	Some Important Early Publications	91

Abbreviations

AB	American Bookman
HLQ	Huntington Library Quarterly
JEGP	Journal of English and Germanic Philology
MLN	Modern Language Notes
MLR	Modern Language Review
MP	Modern Philology
N&Q	Notes and Queries
PMLA	Publications of the Modern Language Association of America
PQ	Philological Quarterly
RAA	Revue Anglo-Américaine
RES	Review of English Studies
RLC	Revue de la littérature comparée
SRL	Saturday Review of Literature
TBR	New York Times Book Review
TLS	London Times Literary Supplement

Laurence Sterne; A List of Critical Studies,
Published from 1896-1946.

I. Bibliography

1. Bartholomew, A. T., "Laurence Sterne," in
   Cambridge history of English Literature,
   New York, 1913, X, pp. 475-476.

2. Block, Andrew, The English novel, 1740-1850.
   A short catalogue..., London, 1939.

3. Cross, Wilbur L., The life and times of Laurence
   Sterne. A new edition, New Haven, Yale
   University press, 1925.
   A detailed list of Sterne's writings appended.
   Rev. Edith Birkhead, MLR, XXI (1926),
   322-24; J. B. Priestley, SRL, Feb. 20,
   1926, 569-70; J. M. Turnball, RES, II
   (1926), 356-60; PQ, V (1926), 370.

4. Curtis, L. P., "Laurence Sterne," in Cambridge
   Bibliography of English literature, New
   York, 1941, II, pp. 521-523.

5. Ryan, M. J., "An edition of Sterne," TLS,
   September 16, 1926, p. 616.

6. Tobin, James E., Eighteenth century literature
   and its cultural background: a bibliography,
   New York, Fordham University press, 1939,
   pp. 160-161.

II. Biography and General Criticism

7. Bagehot, Walter, Literary studies, ed. R. H.
   Hutton., 3v., London, 1905.
   Vol. II contains an article from the National
   Review (April 1864) which expresses righteous
   indignation of mid-Victorians at Sterne's
   "immorality."

Baker, Ernest A., The history of the English   8.
    novel: intellectual realism from Richardson
    to Sterne, London, 1930.

Behrmann, Friedrich, "Samuel Paterson and   9.
    Sterne," N&Q, CLXV (Oct. 7, 1933), 247.

_____, Laurence Sterne und sein einfluss   10.
    auf die englische prosa des achtzehnten
    jahrhunderts, Zürich, 1936.

Benjamin, Lewis S., Some eccentrics and a   11.
    woman, London, 1911.
    Sterne's Eliza.

Bensley, Edward, "Sterne and Lord Aboyne,"   12.
    N&Q, CL (1926), 65-66.

_____, "A debt of Sterne's," TLS, November 1,   13.
    1928, p. 806.

_____, "Laurence Sterne's daughter," N&Q,   14.
    CLXV, (July 15, 1933).

_____, "Laurence Sterne's daughter," N&Q,   15.
    CLXV, (August 5, 1933), 85.

Binz-Winiger, E., Erziehungsfragen in den   16.
    romanen von Richardson, Fielding, Smollett,
    Goldsmith und Sterne, Zürich, 1924.

Birrell, Augustine, "Yorick and Eliza," Nation-   17.
    Athenaeum, XLVI (Dec. 1934), 10, 347-348.

Brown, Herbert R., "Richardson and Sterne in the   18.
    Massachusetts magazine," New England
    magazine, V (1932), 65-82.

Calder-Marshall, A., "Laurence Sterne" in The   19.
    English novelists: a survey of the novel by
    twenty contemporary novelists, London, 1936.

Connolly, Cyril, "Sterne and Swift," Atlantic   20.
    monthly, CLXXV (1945), 94-96.

Cross, Wilbur L., Works of Laurence Sterne,   21.
    12v., New York, 1904.

Laurence Sterne

22. ———, "Laurence Sterne in the twentieth century," Yale review, XV (Oct. 1925), 99-112. Cf. R. Le Gallienne, Lit. digest international book, IV (February 1926), 181-183.

23. Curtis, Lewis P., "Sterne and sentimental," TLS, June 23, 1927, p. 440.

24. ———, The politicks of Laurence Sterne, Oxford, 1929.
Rev. Wilbur Cross, Yale Review, XIX (1929), 181-82; TLS, March 28, 1929, p. 253.

25. ———, "Sterne in Bond Street," TLS, March 24, 1932, p. 17.

26. De Froe, A., Laurence Sterne and his novels studied in the light of modern psychology, Groningen, 1925.
Rev. L. Cazamian, RAA, III (1926), 44-50; B. Fehr, Beiblatt, XXXVI (1925), 289-94; PQ, V (1926), 370.

27. Dernêe, Paul, "Le Révérend Laurence Sterne" Mercure de France, XVI (1913), 539-551.

28. Dibelius, Wilhelm, Englische romankunst. Die technik des englischen romans in achtzehnten und zu anfang des neunzehnten jahrhunderts, 2v., Berlin, 1910.

29. Doernburg, Emil, "W. Raabe und Laurence Sterne", Mitteilungen für die gesellschaft de freunde Wilhelm Raabes, XXIX (1939), 68-71.

30. Eaves, Thomas C. D., Graphic illustration of the principal English novels of the 18th century, [unpublished Harvard University dissertation], 1944, pp. 211-61.

31. A Facsimile reproduction of a unique catalogue of Laurence Sterne's library. With a preface by Charles Whibley, London, 1930.

Fitzgerald, Percy, Life of Laurence Sterne, 2v., 32.
New York, 1904. [2v., London, 1864].
This is a reprint by Cross in #21.

Fluchère, Henri, "Sterne documents," TLS, 33.
February 12, 1925, p. 104.
Announces that he is engaged on a new study
of Sterne.

_____, "Laurence Sterne et William Combe," 34.
RAA, VIII (1931), 313-28.
On Margaret R. B. Shaw's Second Journal
to Eliza. Cf. PQ, IX, 201.

Franz, Heinrich, Laurence Sterne und Edward 35.
Butler, Lord Lytton, Leipzig, 1904.

Galloway, W. F., "Boswell and Sterne," Letters, 36.
V (1931), 21-25, 30.

Glaesener, Henri, "Laurence Sterne," TLS, 37.
May 26, 1927, pp. 361-362.

_____, "Laurence Sterne et Xavier de 38.
Maistre," RLC, VII (1927), 459-479.

Gosse, Edmund, "The bi-centenary of Laurence 39.
Sterne. An address delivered to the
Author's Club, November 24, 1913,"
English review, XVI (1914),
228-234.

Greenwood, Sir George, "Sterne and the verb 40.
to lay," TLS, July 6, 1922.
Cf. R. Pierpoint, ibid., July 13.

Hallamore, Gertrude J., Das bild Laurence 41.
Sternes in Deutschland von der aufklärung
bis zur romantik, Berlin, 1936.

Hartley, Lodwick, This is Lorence: a narrative 42.
of the Reverend Laurence Sterne, Chapel Hill,
University of North Carolina press, 1943.
Rev. Edward Wagenknecht, TBR, June 20,
1943, p. 8; W. B. C. Watkins MLN, LIX
(1943), 363-64; James A. Workin, JEGP,
XLIII (1943), 479-81.

Hirn, Yrjo, Den gamla postvagnen och nagra av dess passagerare, Helsingfors, 1926. Sterne and Borrow. 43.

Jackson, Holbrook, Great English novelists, London, 1908. 44.

Laird, John, "Shandean philosophy," in Philosophical incursions into English literature, pp. 74-91, Cambridge, 1946. 45.

Lohman, F. Louise W. M. Buisman de Savornin, Laurence en de Nederlandse schrijvers van c. 1780-c. 1840, Wageningen, 1939. 46.

Ludwig, Albert, "Zu Dickens und Sterne," Archiv für das studium neuernen sprachen, CLVI (1934), 235-237. 47.

Maack, R., Laurence Sterne in Lichte seiner Zeit, Hamburg, 1936. 48.

Mander, Gerald P., "The shorn lamb," corr. in TLS, July 17, 1937, p. 528. 49.

McCullough, Bruce W., Representative English novelists: Defoe to Conrad, New York, 1946. 50.

Melville, Lewis [Lewis S. Benjamin], Life and letters of Laurence Sterne, 2v., London, 1911. 51.

Montero-Bustamante, Rául, La ciudad de los libros, Montevideo, 1944. Una lectura de Sterne. 52.

More, Paul Elmer, Shelburne essays, Vol. II New York, 1906. 53.

Muir, Edwin, "Laurence Sterne," AB, LXXIII (1930), 1-5. 54.

Myers, Walter, "O, the hobby-horse," Virginia quarterly review, XIX (1943), 268-77. A popular article. 55.

56. Notes and queries, 8th series, III, 165, 213.
    Sterne's marriage.

57. Ibid., 8th series, III, 205.
    Sterne and Pilgrim's Progress.

58. Ibid., 8th series, VI, 6.
    Sterne and plagiarisms.

59. Ibid., 8th series, XII, 264.
    Sterne and two donkeys in literature.

60. Ibid., 9th series, X, 5, 325, 451.
    Inaccurate allusions to Sterne.

61. Ibid., 9th series, XII, 447.
    Fragments in the manner of Sterne.

62. Ibid., 11th series, I, 76, 152.
    Sterne on clothes and their influence.

63. Ibid., 11th series, VI, 375.
    Sterne and Dr. Slop.

64. Ollard, S. L., "Sterne as a young parish priest," TLS, March 18, 1926, p. 217.

65. _____, "Sterne as a parish priest," TLS, May 25, 1933, p. 364.

66. _____, "Sterne as a parish priest," TLS, June 1, 1933, p. 380.

67. Paul, H. W., Men and letters, London, 1901.

68. Pearce, Roy Harvey, "Sterne and sensibility in American diaries," MLN, LIX (1944), 403-407.

69. Pope, Hennesy, Dama Una, "Laurence Sterne," Quarterly review, CCLXVI (1936), 87-101.

70. Powys, Llewelyn, "Laurence Sterne," Bookman, LVIII (Sept. 1923), 10-16.

71. Pottle, F. A., "Bozzy and Yorick," Blackwood's magazine, CCXVII (1925).

Pressly, I. P., "Laurence Sterne" in A York 72.
miscellany, London, 1938, pp. 188-209.
See also the essay on Dr. John Burton,
pp. 141-157.

Putney, Rufus D. S., "Alas, poor Eliza," MLR, 73.
XLI (1946), 411-413.
Argues that Mrs. James, not Eliza Draper,
is the unnamed lady who inspired Sterne's
epitaph of 1767.

Quennell, Peter, Four portraits: studies of the 74.
18th century, London, 1945.

Rabizzani, G., "Lorenzo Sterne," Profili, #31, 75.
Genoa, 1914.

Read, Herbert, The sense of glory, New York, 76.
1929.

Reed, Myrtle, Love affairs of literary men, 77.
New York, 1907.

Reitzel, William, "Cobbett and Sterne," TLS, 78.
December 10, 1931, p. 1006.

Reul, Paul de, Laurence Sterne: cent chefs- 79.
d'oeuvres étrangers, Paris, 1930.

Saintsbury, George, "Laurence Sterne," Bookman, 80.
XLIV (1913), 151-156.

Seligo, Irene, "Der muntere Yorick," Frankfurter 81.
Zeitung, November 27, 1938, p. 6.
On Sterne's 225th birthday.

Sellers, H., "A Sterne problem," TLS, October 21, 82.
1926, p. 722.
Comment by C. Wanklyn, ibid., November 4,
p. 770.

The Shakespeare Head edition of the works of 83.
Laurence Sterne, Oxford: Blackwell, 1927. 7v.

Sichel, Walter, Sterne: a study, London, 1910. 84.

Steinbrecht, Fritz, Der humor bei Laurence 85.
    Sterne, Halle, 1921.
    Summary in Jahrb. d. phil. Fak. Halle-
    Wittenberg, 1920, Part I, 9-12.

Todhunter, John, An essay in search of a subject, 86.
    London, [1904?]

Traill, H. D., Sterne (English men of letters), 87.
    New York, 1909. [1882].

Watkins, W. B. C., "Yorick revisited" in 88.
    Perilous balance, the tragic genius of
    Swift, Johnson and Sterne, Princeton
    University Press, 1939, pp. 99-156.

Whitwell, Elwin, Some XVIIIth century men of 89.
    letters, 2v., London, 1902.

"Yorick at Yale," Yale University library gazette, 90.
    XX (1946), 51-52.
    New materials relating to Sterne.

Yoseloff, Thomas, A fellow of infinite jest, 91.
    New York, 1945.
    Rev. Rufus Putney, PQ, XXV (1946), p. 164.

III. The Life and Opinions
of Tristram Shandy, Gent.

Baird, Theodore, "The time-scheme of Tristram 92.
    Shandy and a source," PMLA, LI (1936),
    803-20.

Bensley, Edward, "An alleged source of Tristram 93.
    Shandy," N&Q, CLIX (1930), 27, 84.
    The life and memoirs of Mr. Ephraim
    Tristram Bates (1756). The article seems
    to have been written in ignorance of Helen
    Sard Hughes's study of the same subject in
    JEGP, XVII 227-251.

Caskey, J. Homer, "Two notes on Uncle Toby," 94.
    MLN, XLII (1927), 321-323.
    Possible borrowings from Edward Moore.

Laurence Sterne

95. Life and opinions of Tristram Shandy, gentleman by Laurence Sterne, Introduction by Wilbur L. Cross. New York [1925].

96. Curtis, Lewis P., "The first printer of Tristram Shandy," PMLA, XLVII (1932), 777-789. The first edition of the first two volumes of Tristram Shandy were printed at York by Ann Ward.

97. Eaves, T. C. Duncan, "George Romney: his Tristram Shandy paintings and trip to Lancaster," HLQ, VII (1944), 321-326.

98. Eddy, William A., "Tom Brown and Tristram Shandy," MLN, XLIV (1929), 379-381.

99. Hine, Reginald L., "Captain Robert Hinds," TLS, May 21, 1931, p. 408. A supposed original of Uncle Toby.

100. Hughes, Helen S., "A precursor of Tristram Shandy," JEGP, XVII (1918), 227-251. See, in this connexion, #93.

101. Lehman, B. H., "Of time, personality, and the author. A study of Tristram Shandy: comedy," Studies in the comic, University of California studies in English, Vol. VIII, #2, 1941, pp. 233-250.

102. Life and opinions of Tristram Shandy, gentlemen... Introduction by Christopher Morley. New York, 1935.

103. Notes and Queries, 8th series, II, 304, 372, 494. Obscenity in Tristram Shandy.

104. Ibid., 8th series, III, 36. Obscenity in Tristram Shandy.

105. Ibid., 8th series, VII, 28. A mistake in Tristram Shandy.

106. Ibid., 11th series, XI, 67, 192. An allusion in Tristram Shandy.

Ibid., 11th series, XI, 188.   107.
    Confucius in Tristram Shandy.

Priestley, J. B., "The brothers Shandy" in   108.
    The English comic characters, London, 1925.

Russell, H. K., "Tristram Shandy and the technique   109.
    of the novel," SP, XLII (1945), 581-593.

TLS, February 22, 1934, p. 132.   110.
    Bibliographical notes on Tristram Shandy.

Tompkins, J. M. S., "Triglyph and Tristram,"   111.
    TLS, July 11, 1929, p. 558.
    Allusions to Sterne by Richard Griffith.

Turnbull, John M., "The prototype of Walter   112.
    Shandy's Tristrapoedia," RES, II (1926), 212-215.

Urbahn, Therese, "Die Geste in Sternes Tristram   113.
    Shandy," Britannica, XII (1936), 171-87.

Work, James A., "Tristram Shandy," corr. in   114.
    TLS, September 4, 1937, p. 640.

_____, ed., The life and opinions of Tristram   115.
    Shandy, gentleman. Odyssey series in
    literature, New York, 1940.
    The first reprint of the first London edition
    of the nine volumes which had Sterne's super-
    vision through the press, with Hogarth's
    illustrations and facsimiles of title-pages.
    Illuminating and thorough introduction.

IV. A Sentimental Journey Through France and Italy

A Sentimental journey through France and Italy.   116.
    Introduction by Francis Beckley. London, 1922.

A Sentimental journey through France and Italy...   117.
    Introduction by Wilbur L. Cross. New York, 1926.
    Selections from the Journals, Sermons and
    Correspondence as well.

Laurence Sterne

Murakami, Shiko, "On the Sentimental Journey," 118.
 Studies in English literature, Imperial
 University of Tokyo, XV (1934), 345-359.

Notes and Queries, 8th series, I, 228-300. 119.
 Smellfungus and Mundungus.

Putney, Rufus, "The evolution of A Sentimental 120.
 Journey," PQ, XIX (1940), 349-369.

A sentimental journey through France and Italy. 121.
 Introduction by Herbert Read. London,
 Scholartis press, 1929.
 Rev. A. Birrell, Nation-Athenaeum, XLIV
 (1929), 22.

A sentimental journey through France and Italy. 122.
 Introduction by Virginia Woolf. Oxford, 1928.

V. The Letters

Laurence Sterne's letter to Rev. Mr. Blake. 123.
 Privately printed from original in possession
 of William K. Bixby. St. Louis, 1915.

Clark, Edwin, "Sterne's letters are a mystery," 124.
 TBR, January 15, 1928, pp. 1, 25.

Curtis, Lewis P., "Forged letters of Laurence 125.
 Sterne," PMLA, L (1935), 1076-1106.

_____, ed., Letters of Laurence Sterne. 126.
 Oxford: Clarendon press, 1935.
 Rev. TLS, March 21, 1935, p. 173; Corr.
 by Margaret R. B. Shaw, ibid., June 6,
 1935, p. 364.

Fluchère, Henri, "Sterne épistolier," RAA, 127.
 XIII (1936), 297-310.

Sclater, W. L., "Letters addressed by Eliza 128.
 Draper to the Strange Family, 1776-1778,"
 N&Q, CLXXXVI (1944), 201-204, 220-224.

_____, "Letters addressed by Eliza Draper 129.
 to the Strange family, 1776-1778," N&Q,
 CLXXXVII (1944), 7-13, 27-33, 48-54.

Second journal to Eliza. By Laurence Sterne. 130.
Hitherto known as Letters supposed to have been written by Yorrick and Eliza, but now shown to be a later version of the Journal to Eliza. Transcribed from the copy in the British Museum and presented with an introduction by Margaret R. B. Shaw, together with a forward by Charles Whibley. London, 1929.
Rev. E. E. K., New Statesman, November 9, 1929, p. viii; Wilbur L. Cross, SRL, December 21, 1929, p. 587 (rejects the ascription); TLS, October 31, 1929, p. 867.

VI. Foreign Influence and Reputation

Baker, T. S., "The influence of Laurence Sterne upon German literature," German-American annuals, II (1898-1899), pp. 41-56. 131.

Barton, Francis B., L'Influence de Sterne en France, Paris, 1911. 132.

―――――, "Laurence Sterne and Charles Nodier," MP, XIV (1917). 133.

―――――, "Laurence Sterne and Théophile Gautier," MP, XVI (1918). 134.

Behmer, Carl A., Laurence Sterne und C. M. Wieland, Munchen, 1899. 135.

Czerney, Johann, Sterne, Hippel und Jean Paul, Berlin, 1904. 136.

Hayes, Joseph C., Laurence Sterne and Jean Paul, Abridgement of thesis (Ph.D.), New York University, New York, 1939. 137.

Klingemann, Gisbert, Goethe's verhältnis zu Laurence Sterne, Marburg, 1929. 138.

Longo, Joseph, Laurence Sterne und Johann Jacobi, Vienna, 1898. 139.

Laurence Sterne

140. Lussky, Alfred Edwen, <u>Tieck's romantic irony with special emphasis upon the influence of Cervantes, Sterne, and Goethe,</u> Chapel Hill: University of North Carolina press, 1932.

141. Pinger, Wilhelm, <u>Laurence Sterne und Goethe,</u> Berkeley, 1920.

142. Price, L. M., <u>English and German literary influences,</u> Berkeley, 1920.

143. Rabizzani, G., <u>Sterne in Italia,</u> Rome, 1920.

144. Sears, Charles Baldwin, "The literary influence of Sterne in France," <u>PMLA,</u> XVII (1902), 221-236.

145. Thayer, Harvery W. Hewett, <u>Sterne in Germany,</u> New York, 1905.

146. Vocano, Stefan, <u>Heine und Sterne,</u> Berlin, 1907.

VII. Miscellaneous

147. Cross, Wilbur L., ed., <u>A Political romance</u> (1759), Boston, 1914.

148. Curtis, Lewis P., "The printer of Sterne's Political Romance," <u>TLS,</u> February 28, 1935, p. 163.

149. Wright, A., and Slater, W. L., ed., <u>Eliza; some account of her life in India,</u> London, 1922.

VIII. Some Important Early Publications

150. Ferriar, J., <u>Illustrations of Sterne,</u> London, 1798.

151. Stapfer, P., <u>Laurence Sterne: sa personne et ses ouvrages,</u> Paris, 1870.

152. "Traditions of Sterne and Bunyan," <u>Macmillan's magazine,</u> XXVIII (1873).

153. "Some memorials of Laurence Sterne," <u>Athenaeum,</u> March 30, 1878.

Merwin, H. C., "Philosophy of Sterne," 154.
    Atlantic Monthly, LXXIV (1894).

V.

Henry Fielding
a List of Critical Studies
Published from 1895 to 1946

Copyright 1948 by Francesco Cordasco

Preface

There is no guide to Fielding criticism; at best the researcher may turn to the CBEL, which contains a selective list, or to the monumental work of Cross (see #5 in compilation) which gives only a list of the works. Yet, Fielding criticism has been rich and significant. Two hundred years have passed since the appearance of Tom Jones, and the interest in Fielding and his versatile genius continues. In this list every care has been taken to include all studies which, in one manner or another, have dealt with Fielding from 1895 to 1946. These fifty years have been particularly important in Fielding scholarship: the novels have been carefully edited, much obscure biographic detail has been cleared, and Fielding has received his measure of attention as important essayist and dramatist.

It has been thought advisable to divide the list under headings of bibliography, biography, general criticism, and individual works, rather than to have incorporated all entries in one alphabetical enumeration. Cross reference indicates important corroborative or dissident opinion. Reviews have been noticed only when they assume important critical stature. The reader is advised to consult further the Annual bibliography of English language and literature (Modern Humanities Research Association, 1920-date); Year's work in English studies (English Association, 1921-date); English literature, 1660-1800; A current bibliography (Philological quarterly, 1926-date).

F. C.

Contents

I.	Bibliography	99
II.	Biography	101
III.	Criticism: General and Literary	104
IV.	Shamela Andrews	110
V.	Joseph Andrews	111
VI.	Jonathan Wild	111
VII.	Tom Jones	112
VIII.	Amelia	114
IX.	Periodical Writings	114
X.	Plays	115
XI.	Miscellaneous	117
XII.	Some Important Early Publications	117

Abbreviations

CBEL	Cambridge bibliography of English literature (4v, 1941)
ELH	Journal of English literary history
JEGP	Journal of English and Germanic philology
LM	London Mercury
MLN	Modern language notes
MLQ	Modern language quarterly
MLR	Modern language review
N&Q	Notes and queries
MP	Modern philology
PMLA	Publications of the Modern language association
PQ	Philological quarterly
RAA	Revue anglo-américaine
RES	Review of English studies
SP	Studies in philology
SRL	Saturday review of literature
TLS	London Times literary supplement

Henry Fielding: a list of critical studies, published from 1895 to 1946.

I. Bibliography

Baker, Ernest A., <u>The history of the English novel: intellectual realism from Richardson to Sterne,</u> London, 1930.
Brief bibliography, pp. 278-279.   1.

Chandler, Knox, "Two Fielding Pamphlets," <u>PQ</u>, XVI (1937), 410-12.   2.

Child, H. H., <u>Cambridge history of English literature,</u> New York, 1913, X, pp. 413-18.   3.

Coolidge, Archibald, "A Fielding pamphlet?", <u>TLS,</u> May 9, 1936, p. 400.   4.

Cross, Wilbur L., <u>The history of Henry Fielding,</u> 3v., New Haven, 1918, III, 289-366.   5.
    I. Fielding's published works.
    II. Uncertain or doubtful authorship.
    III. Works erroneously attributed to Fielding.
    IV. Dramas on Fielding or his works.
    V. Letters and manuscripts.

deCastro, J. P., "The printing of Fielding's works," <u>Library,</u> 4th ser., I, March (1921), 257-70.   6.

_____, "Fielding Manuscripts," <u>TLS,</u> June 1, 1940, p. 267.   7.

Dickson, F. S., "Biographies of Fielding" in Thomas Keightly, <u>The life and writings of Henry Fielding</u> (ed. F. S. Dickson) Cleveland, 1907.   8.

_____, Fielding's dramatic works...a list of   9.

the different editions of his plays, Phila., 1912.

———, "The early editions of Fielding's Voyage to Lisbon," Library, VIII (1917), 29-35.
Cf. Pollard, Ibid., 75-77; deCastro, Ibid., pp. 145-159.
   10.

Digeon, Aurélien, Le texte des romans de Fielding: étude critique, Paris, 1923.
   11.

Dobson, Austin, "Henry Fielding," Bibliographica, I (1895), 163-173.
   12.

Gill, W. W., "Early Fielding documents," N&Q, CLXXI (1936), 242.
   13.

Henley, W. E., et al., "A bibliographic list of first editions" in Works of Henry Fielding, 16v., N. Y., 1903, XVI, xlvii-lxii.
   14.

Hughes, Helen S., "A dialogue - possibly by Fielding," PQ, I (1922), 49-55.
   15.

Jarvis, R. C., "The death of Walpole: Henry Fielding and a forgotten cause célèbre," MLR, XLI (1946), 113-30.
The ascription of a pamphlet to Fielding.
   16.

Jensen, Gerald E., "An address to the electors of Great Britain...Possibly a Fielding tract," MLN, XL (1925), 57-58.
   17.

Locke, Miriam, A., "An edition of the True Patriot by Henry Fielding with an introduction and critical notes," Summaries of doctoral dissertations, Northwestern University, XIII (1945), 9-14.
   18.

Mead, Herman R., "Variant issues of The Coffeehouse Politicians (1730)," Papers of the bibliographical society of America, XXXV (1941), 69.
   19.

Rice-Oxley, L., "Henry Fielding" in CBEL, II, 517-520.
   20.

Henry Fielding

21. Seymour, Mabel, "Henry Fielding," LM, XXIV (1931), 160.
Bibliographical notes on A compleat and authentick history of the rise, progress, and extinction of the late rebellion.

22. Tobin, James E., Eighteenth century English literature and its cultural background: a bibliography, N. Y., Fordham Univ. press, 1939.

23. Vincent, Howard P., "Early poems by Henry Fielding," N&Q, CLXXXIV (1943), 159-60.
The text of two poems.

24. Wallace, Robert M., "Fielding manuscripts," TLS, May 18, 1940, p. 243.
See #7.

25. Wagenknecht, Edward, Cavalcade of the English novel, N. Y., 1943.
Brief bibliography, p. 587.

II. Biography

26. Blanchard, Frederic T., Fielding the novelist., New Haven, 1925.
Cf. PQ, V (1926), 360; Ibid., VI (1927), 180. See reviews: E. A. Baker, RES, III (1927), 227-32; F. Baldensperger, Litteris, IV (1927), 222-25; P. Dottin, RELV, XLIII (1926), 450-55; O. Elton, MLR, XXII (1927), 225-28; A. Digeon, RAA, V (1927), 57-59; E. S. Noyes, SRL, Oct. 16, 1926, p. 198; H. Schojjer, Beiblatt, XXXVIII (1927), 345-96.

27. Banerji, H. K., Henry Fielding: playwright, journalist and master of the art of fiction, his life and his works. Oxford, 1929.
Cf. PQ, X (April, 1931), 200-201. See reviews: A. Digeon, RAA, VII (1930), 62; E. G. Twitchett, LM, XXI (1930), 373-75; TLS, April 3, 1930 p. 293.

28. C_____, T. C., "Fielding and Bentley," N&Q, CLXXXVI (1944), 245-46.

Cross, Wilbur L., The history of Henry Fielding, 29.
3v., New Haven, 1918.
See #5; reviews: N&Q 12th series, VIII,
181-185; Revue germanique, Oct.-Dec.,
XIII (1922), 412-17.

deCastro, J. P., "Edmund Fielding," N&Q, 30.
August 26, XI (1922), 178.
Fielding's father. See #26, #27, #29.

_____, "Fielding and Lyme Regis," TLS, 31.
June 4, 1931, p. 447.

Dobson, Austin, "Fielding's Library" in 18th 32.
century vignettes, series 3, London, 1896.

_____, Henry Fielding: a memoir, N. Y., 33.
1900.

_____, Henry Fielding (English men of 34.
letters), London, 1907.

_____, Fielding and Andrew Millar, 35.
London, 1916.

Dorothy, George M., "The sale of Fielding's 36.
farm," TLS, June 26, 1924.

DuBois, Arthur E., "A forgotten Salisbury 37.
surgeon," TLS, March 19, 1931.
See comment by J. P. deCastro, Ibid.,
March 26, p. 252.

Elwin, W., Some 18th century men of letters, 38.
2v., London, 1902.

Godden, G. M., Henry Fielding: a memoir, 39.
London, 1910.
Newly discovered letters and records;
illustrations from contemporary prints.

Jones, B. Maelor, Henry Fielding, novelist and 40.
magistrate, London, 1933.
Review: TLS, July 20, 1933, p. 493; see
corrections, A. R. Leslie-Melville, Ibid.,
July 27, p. 572; J. P. deCastro,
Ibid., August 10, p. 537.

Keightly, Thomas, Life and writings of Henry 41.
    Fielding (ed. F. S. Dickson), Cleveland,
    1907.
    See # 8.

McKillop, Alan D., "The personal relations be- 42.
    tween Fielding and Richardson," MP,
    XXVIII (1931), 423-33.

Nichols, C. W., "Fielding and the Cibbers," 43.
    PQ, I (1922), 278-89.

Notes and queries, 8th series, IV, 164, 314. 44.
    An inscription on Fielding

Ibid., 9th series, I, 168. 45.
    Fielding's house at Canterbury.

Ibid., 9th series, VII, 248-249. 46.
    Fielding and Brillat-Savarin.

Ibid., 9th series, XII, 65. 47.
    Fielding and Fordhook House, Uxbridge Road.

Ibid., 10th series, VI, 47. 48.
    Fielding's first marriage at Charlcombe
    Church.

Ibid., 10th series, IX, 49, 134, 277. 49.
    Inscription on Fielding's grave.

Ibid., 11th series, III, 486; IV, 58, 277, 336, 50.
    419, 534.
    Fielding and the civil power, 1751.

Ibid., 11th series, XI, 301. 51.
    Fielding and Sarah Andrew, 1725.

Ibid., 11th series, XII, 300, 351, 408. 52.
    Portraits of Fielding.

Ibid., 12th series, I, 264. 53.
    Fielding at Boswell Court, c. 1745.

Ibid., 12th series, II, 104. 54.
    Fielding and the Collier family.

Ibid., 12th series, II, 11. 55.
Fielding and John Ranby.

Ibid., 12th series, III, 469. 56.
Fielding's birthplace.

Ibid., 12th series, VI, 34. 57.
Fielding's ancestors at Sharpham Part,
Somerset.

Swaen, A. E. H., "Fielding and Goldsmith at 58.
Leyden," MLR, I (1906).

Saintsbury, George, Fielding, London, 1909. 59.

Vincent, Howard P., "The childhood of Henry 60.
Fielding," RES, XVI (1940), 438-44.

_____, "Henry Fielding in prison," MLR, 61.
XXXVI (1941), 499-500.

Voorde, F. P. van de, Henry Fielding, critic 62.
and satirist, Gravenhage, 1931.

III. Criticism: General and Literary

Alain, M., "En lisant Fielding," La nouvelle 63.
revue française, LII (1939), 484-91.

Baker, E. A., History of the English novel: 64.
intellectual realism from Richardson
to Sterne, London, 1930.
See #1.

Beatty, Richard C., "Criticism in Fielding's 65.
narratives and his estimate of critics,"
PMLA, XLIX (1934), 1087-1100.

Becker, Gustav, "Die Bedeutung des Wortes 66.
romantic bei Fielding und Smollett,"
Archiv für das studium der neueren
sprachen und literaturen, CX (1903),
pp. 56-66.

Binz-Winiger, E., Erziehungsfragen in den 67.
romanen von Richardson, Fielding, Smollett,
Goldsmith und Sterne, Zurich, 1926.

68. Birkhead, E., Sentiment and sensibility in the 18th century novel (Essays and studies by members of the English association), London, 1925.

69. Birrell, A., More obiter dicta, N. Y., 1896.

70. Bissell, Frederick O., Fielding's theory of the novel, Cornell Univ. Press, 1933.
Notice in TLS, August 3, 1933, p. 526.

71. Blanchard, Frederic T., "Coleridge's estimate of Fielding" in Gayley anniversary papers, pp. 153-63.

72. Brown, Jack R., "From Aaron Hill to Henry Fielding," PQ, XVIII (1939), 85-88.

73. Chandler, Frank W., Literature of roguery, 2v., Boston, 1907.

74. Cross, Wilbur R., Development of the English novel, N. Y., 1899.

75. _____, "A new estimate of Fielding," SRL, L (July 18, 1925), 905-906.

76. deCastro, J. P., "Gravelot," N&Q, CLXXX (1941), 87.
But see C. H. Crouch, Ibid., p. 107; on H. F. Bourguignon, illustrator of the French translation of Tom Jones.

77. _____, "Derham," N&Q, CLXXX (1941), 123.
Identifies Mr. Derham, of A journal of a voyage to Lisbon.

78. Dibelius, W., Englische Romankunst. Die technik des englischen Romans in achtzehnten und zu anfang des neuzehnten Jahrhunderts, 2v., Berlin, 1910.
See JEGP, II (1912), pp. 626-35.

79. Digeon, A., Les romans de Fielding, Paris 1923. (Eng. trans. 1925).
See reviews: F. T. Blanchard, Univ. of Calif. chronicles, XXVIII (1926). 105-07;

S. B. Liljegren, Litteris, III (1926), 103-04.

80. _____, "Autour de Fielding," Revue germanique, XI (1920).

81. _____, "Fielding a-t-il écrit le dernier chapitre de A journey from this world into the next?", RAA, VIII (1931), 428-30.
Attributes it to Sarah Fielding.

82. Dobson, Austin, "Fielding Find," National review, LVIII (1911).

83. _____, "A new dialogue of the dead," Rosalba's journal, London, 1915.
Corrects errors of Murphy.

84. Düber, R., Beiträge zu Henry Fieldings romantechnik, Halle, 1910.

85. Ernle, Lord, "Founders of the modern novel," Edinburgh review, CCXLIII (1926), 336-54.

86. Esdaile, Mrs., "Fielding's Danish translator: Simon Charles Stanley, the sculptor," TLS, April 3, 1937, p. 252.
Cf. correspondence, B. Rockham, Ibid., April 17, p. 292.

87. Ewald, Eugen, Abbild und wunschbild der gesellschaft bei Richardson und Fielding, Wuppertal, 1935.

88. Fischer, Hildegard, Das subjectiv element in den romanen Fieldings, Ohlau, 1933.

89. Frohlich, R. A., Fieldings humor in seinen romanen, Leipzig, 1918.

90. Glenn, S. E., "Some French influences on Henry Fielding," Abstracts of theses, University of Illinois, 1932.

91. Gosse, Edmund, ed., Works of Henry Fielding, 12v., 1898-99.
Critical introductions.

Henry Fielding

92. Habel, U., Die Nachwirkung des picaresken romans in England, von Nash bis Fielding und Smollett. Breslau, 1930.

93. Hammond, Geraldine E., "Evidence of the dramatist's technique in Henry Fielding's novels," Bulletin of the Univ. of Wichita, XVI, #10, 1941.

94. Heidler, J. B., History, from 1700-1800, of English criticism of prose fiction, Urbana (Illinois), s. d.

95. Heilman, Robert B., "Fielding and 'the first Gothic revival'," MLN, LVII (1942), 671-73.

96. Hill, Rowland M., "Setting in the novels of Henry Fielding," Bulletin of the Citadel, VII (1943), 26-51.

97. ———, "Jonathan Wild," TLS, August 14, 1943, p. 396.
Argues that A journey from this world to the next and Jonathan Wild are Fielding's first efforts in fiction, although Joseph Andrews preceeded them in order of publication. But see Brian W. Downs in TLS, Sept. 11, 1943, p. 444.

98. Homann, Wilhelm, Henry Fielding als humorist, Marburg, 1900.

99. Huffmann, C. H., The 18th century novel in theory and practice, Dayton, [1920].

100. Hughes, Helen S., "Fielding's indebtedness to James Ralph," MP, XX (1922), 19-34.

101. Hughes, Leo, "The influence of Fielding's milieu upon his humor" Studies in English... University of Texas, 1944, pp. 269-297.

102. Humphreys, A. R., "Fielding's irony: its methods and effects," RES, XVIII (1942), 183-96.
See PQ, XXII (April, 1943), 158.

Irwin, W. R., "Satire and comedy in the works of Henry Fielding," ELH, XIII (1946), 168-188.
Development of Fielding's comic spirit. 103.

Jensen, G. E., "Fashionable society in Fielding's time," PMLA, XXXI (1916), 79-89. 104.

_____, "A Fielding discovery," Yale University library gazette, X (1935), 23-32. 105.

Joesten, Maria, Die philosophie Fieldings, Leipzig, 1932.
Fielding's works in terms of Stoicism. See PQ, XII (1933), p. 116. 106.

Liljegren, S. B., "Fielding's charge to the jury, 1745," TLS, March 4, 1926, p. 168.
See #79. 107.

Lind, Levi R., "Lucian and Fielding," Classical weekly, XXIX (1936), 84-86. 108.

Lücker, Heinz, Die verwendung der mundart im englischen romans des 18. jahrhunderts, Darmstadt, 1915. 109.

Maynadier, G. H., ed., Works of Henry Fielding, 12v., N. Y., 1903.
Critical introduction. 110.

Notes and queries, 10th series, V, 446.
A poem by Fielding. 111.

Ibid., 10th series, VII, 444.
Fielding and Shakespeare. 112.

Ibid., 11th series, X, 91, 214.
Fielding's letters. 113.

Ibid., 12th series, III, 7.
Fielding's and Richardson's work on the Continent. 114.

Ibid., 12th series, V., 283.
Fielding as publicist. 115.

Obrier, M., A study of the comic elements in Fielding's novels, Ms. thesis for Diplôme d'études supérieures, University of Paris (Sorbonne), 1922.   116.

Olybrius, "A presentation inscription by Fielding," N&Q, CLXXVIII (1940), 298. But see Ibid., J. P. deCastro, pp. 337-39.   117.

Price, Lawrence M., "The works of Fielding on the German stage, 1762-1801," JEGP, XLI (1942), 257-78.   118.

Prinsen, J., De roman in de 18e Euw in West Europa, Groningen, 1925.   119.

Proper, C. B. A., Social elements in English prose fiction between 1700-1832, Amsterdam, 1929.   120.

Radtke, Bruno, Henry Fielding als Kritiker, Leipzig, 1926. See PQ, VI (1927), 180.   121.

Roberts, W., "Henry Fielding in French," National review, LXXIX (July, 1922), 723-28.   122.

Rogers, Winfield H., "Fielding's early aesthetic and technique," SP, XL (1943), 529-51.   123.

Ronte, Heinz, Richardson und Fielding, Leipzig, 1935.   124.

Saintsbury, George, The English novel, London, 1913.   125.

Schonzler, Heinrich, Fieldings verhältnis zu Le Sage und zu anderen quellen, Weimar, 1915.   126.

Seymour, Mabel, "Fielding's history of the forty-five," PQ, XIV (1935), 105-25.   127.

Stephen, Leslie, Hours in a library, II, N. Y., 1907.   128.

Studt, Annelise, "Fielding's charakterromane," 129.
 Britannica, XIII (1936), 101-18.

Taylor, Houghton W., "Fielding upon Cibber," 130.
 MP, XXIX (1931), 73-90.

Thornbury, Ethel M., Henry Fielding's theory 131.
 of the comic prose epic, University of
 Wisconsin studies in language and literature,
 # 30, Madison, 1931.
 See reviews: A. W. Secord, JEGP, XXXII
 (1933), 417-18; J. R. Sutherland, RES, IX
 (1933), 342-43; G. Kitchin, MLR, XXVIII
 (1933), 110-11.

Tillett, Nettie S., "Is Coleridge indebted to 132.
 Fielding?", SP, XLIII (1946), 675-81.
 Certain views in Biographia literaria.

V_____, E. H., "A curious double parallel 133.
 between Milton and Fielding," N&Q,
 CLXXVI (1939), 260.

Van Doren, Carl, "The greatest English man 134.
 of letters," The nation, June 6, 1923,
 659-60.

Williams, H., Two centuries of the English novel, 135.
 London, 1911.

Wilson, F. W., Dickens in seinen beziehungen 136.
 zu den humoristen Fielding und Smollett,
 Leipzig, 1899.

IV. Shamela Andrews

deCastro, J. P., "Did Fielding write Shamela," 137.
 N&Q, January 8, 1916.

Downs, Brian, W., ed., An apology for the life 138.
 of Mrs. Shamela Andrews, Cambridge, 1930.
 Critical introduction.

Greene, Charles, R., "A note on the authorship 139.
 of Shamela," MLN, LIX (1944), 571.

Johnson, R. Brimely, ed., An apology for the life of Mrs. Shamela Andrews, London, 1926.
Critical introduction; see PQ, VI (April 1927), 179-180.   140.

Woods, Charles, B., "Fielding and the authorship of Shamela," PQ, XXV (1946), 248-72.
Argument's for authorship. But see #137, #139.   141.

V. Joseph Andrews

Bosdorf, Erich, Entstehungsgeshichte von Fieldings Joseph Andrews, Weimar, 1908.   142.

deCastro, J. P., ed., The adventures of Joseph Andrews, London, Scholartis press, 1929.
See reviews: A. Digeon, RAA, VII (1930), 263; N&Q, CLVI (1929), 342; TLS, April 25, 1929, p. 343.   143.

――――, "Fielding's Parson Adams," N&Q March 18, 1916.   144.

Priestley, J. B., "Parson Adams" in The English comic character, London, 1925.   145.

VI. Jonathan Wild

Bispham, G. T., "Fielding's Jonathan Wild" in Eighteenth century literature, Oxford, 1909.   146.

Clark, Charles M., ed., The life of Jonathan Wild the great, (Cornell university abstract of theses, 1942), Cornell university press, 1943.   147.

Irwin, William Robert, The making of "Jonathan Wild": a study in the literary method of Henry Fielding, Columbia university press, 1941.
See review: James A. Work, MLQ, III, 482-84.   148.

Notes and queries, 11th series, II, 261. 149.
    Fielding's Jonathan Wild.

Wells, J. E., "Fielding's political purpose in 150.
Jonathan Wild," PMLA, XXVIII (1913),
1-55.

VII. Tom Jones

deCastro, J. P., "Ursula Fielding and 'Tom 151.
Jones'," N&Q, CLXXVIII (1940), 164-67.

Digeon, A., "La condemnation de Tom Jones 152.
à Paris," RAA, IV (1927), 529-31.

Eaves, T. C. Duncan, "The publication of the 153.
first translations of Fielding's Tom Jones,"
Library, 4th series, XXVI (1945), 189-190.

Haage, Richard, "Charakterzeichnung und 154.
komposition in Fieldings Tom Jones in
ihrer beziehung zum drama," Britannica,
XIII (1936), 119-70.

Iyengar, K. R., "Fielding's Tom Jones," 155.
Journal of the university of Bombay,
VIII, ii (1939), 29-44.

Jensen, G. E., "Proposals for a definitive 156.
edition of Tom Jones," Library, XVIII
(1937), 314-30.

Loomis, R. S., "Tom Jones and Tom-Mania," 157.
Sewanee review, XXVII (1919), 478-95.

McKillop, Alan D., "An iconographic poem on 158.
Tom Jones," PQ, XVII (1938), 403-06.

Mundy, P. D., "Fielding's Tom Jones," N&Q, 159.
CLXIX (1935), 456.
A contemporary letter regarding its
publication.

Nation, LXXXVII (December 24, 1908), 624. 160.
    A bibliographical note.

Henry Fielding

Notes and queries, 9th series, I, 147, 175. Tom Jones in France.	161.
Ibid., 10th series, XII, 407. Tom Jones in French.	162.
Ibid., 11th series, III, 289. "Dowdy" in Tom Jones.	163.
Ibid., 11th series, VI, 348, 470. Parson Thwackum.	164.
Ibid., 11th series, IX, 425, 520. Chronology of Tom Jones.	165.
Ibid., 11th series, IX, 507. Typographical slip in Tom Jones.	166.
Ibid., 11th series, X, 85. Crypic utterance in Tom Jones.	167.
Ibid., 11th series, X, 191, 253, 292, 372. Geography of Tom Jones.	168.
Ibid., 11th series, X, 209, 293, 392. Sack and the unusual words in Tom Jones.	169.
Ibid., 11th series, XI, 12, 56, 60. Geography of Tom Jones. See # 168.	170.
Ibid., 12th series, I, 506. Tom Jones and his sword.	171.
Ibid., 12th series, V, 268, 303, 327; VI, 23, 118. Gibbon's prophecy about Tom Jones.	172.
Van Doren, Carl, "Tom Jones and Philip Carey," Century, CX (May, 1925), 115-120.	173.
Waldschmidt, C., Die dramatiseierungen von Fieldings Tom Jones, Wetzlar, 1906.	174.

VIII. Amelia

McCutcheon, Roger P., "Amelia, or the distressed wife," MLN, XLII (1927), 32-33.   175.

Sherburn, George, "Fielding's Amelia: an interpretation," ELH, III (1936), 1-14.   176.

IX. Periodical Writings

Dobson, Austin, "The Covent Garden Journal" in Sidewalk studies, London, 1902.   177.

Graham, Walter, English literary periodicals, N. Y., 1930.   178.

_____, "The date of The Champion," TLS, February 4, 1932, p. 76.   179.

_____, "The date of The Champion," N&Q, CLXIII (1932), 150-51.   180.

Kohler, Friedrich, Fieldings wochenschrift "The Champion" und das englische leben der zeit, Munster, 1928.   181.

Marr, G. S., The periodical essayists of the 18th century, London, 1923.   182.

Newlin, C. M., "The English periodicals and the novel, 1709-40", Michigan academy of science papers, XVI (1931).   183.

Notes and queries, 12th series, I, 284. Corrections in Covent Garden Journal.   184.

Wells, John E., "Henry Fielding and The Crisis," MLN, XXVII (1912), 18-31.   185.

_____, "The Champion and some unclaimed essays by Henry Fielding," Englische studien, XLVI (1912-13), 355-66.   186.

_____, "Fielding's Champion and Captain Hercules Vinegar," MLR, VIII (1913), 165-72.   187.

_____, "Fielding's miscellanies," MLR, 188.
XIII (1918), 481-82.

_____, "Fielding's Champion - more notes," 189.
MLN, XXXV (1920), 18-23.

X. Plays

Avery, Emmett L., "An early performance of 190.
Fielding's Historical Register, MLN,
XLIX (1934), 407.

_____, "Some notes on Fielding's plays," 191.
Research studies of the State College of
Washington (Pullman, Washington), III
(1935), 48-50.

_____, "Fielding's Universal Gallant," 192.
Research studies of State College of
Washington, VI (1938), 46.

_____, "Fielding's last season with the 193.
Haymarket theatre," MP, XXXVI (1939),
283-92.

Bateson, Frederick N. W., English comic 194.
drama, 1700-1750, Oxford, 1929.

Bookman's journal, XII (August, 1925), 205. 195.
Bibliographical notes on The Female
Husband.

_____, XII (Sept. 1925), 245. 196.
Bibliographical notes on The Female
Husband.

Brown, Jack R., "Four plays by Henry Fielding," 197.
Summaries of doctoral dissertations,
Northwestern university, V (1937), 5-9.

Jaggard, William, "Revivals of Fielding's 198.
plays," N&Q, CLXXX (1941), 15.
Cf. J. D. Rolleston, Ibid., p. 70.

Lindner, F., Henry Fieldings dramatische 199.
werke, Leipzig, 1895.

Nichols, C. W., "Date of Tumble-Down Dick," 200.
MLN, XXXVI (1921), 312-313.

―――――, "Fielding's Tumble-Down Dick," 201.
MLN, XXXVIII (1923), 410-16.

―――――, "Social satire in Fielding's Pasquin 202.
and The Historical Register, PQ, III (1924).

―――――, "Fielding's satire on pantomine," 203.
PMLA, XLVI (1931), 1107-12.

Notes and queries, 12th series, VIII, 184. 204.
The Female Husband.

Ohnsorg, R., John Lacys Dumb Lady, Mrs. 205.
Centilvre's Love's Contrivance und Henry
Fieldings Mock Doctor in ihrem verhältnis
zu einander und zu ihrer gemeinschaftlichen
quellen, Hamburg, 1900.

Parfitt, G. E., L'influence française dans les 206.
oeuvres de Fielding et dans le théatre
anglais contemporain de ses comédies,
Paris, 1928.

Read, Stanley E., "Fielding's Miser," Huntington 207.
library bulletin, I (May 1931), 211-13.

Rogers, Winfield H., "The significance of Fielding's 208.
Temple Beau," PMLA, LV (1940), 440-44.

Stonehill, Charles, "Fielding's The Miser," TLS, 209.
October 22, 1925, p. 698.
Cf. #207.

Woods, Charles B., "Studies in the dramatic 210.
works of Henry Fielding," Harvard university summaries of theses (1935-37),
292-94.

―――――, "Notes on three of Fielding's plays," 211.
PMLA, LII (1937), 359-73.
On The Letter Writers (1731), The Modern
Husband (1732), Eurydice Hiss'd (1737).

Henry Fielding

XI. Miscellaneous

Notes and queries, 9th series, II, 426. 212.
    Names of characters in the novels.

Ibid., 10th series, VI, 61, 115. 213.
    Journal of a voyage to Lisbon.

Ibid., 12th series, I, 284; II, 515. 214.
    Corrections in Voyage to Lisbon.

Ibid., 12th series, III, 100. 215.
    Some date corrections.

Roberts, W., "A shelf of eighteenth century 216.
    novels," Book collectors' quarterly,
    July, 1934.

Streeter, H. W., The 18th century English 217.
    novel in French translation, N. Y., 1936.

Utter, R. P., and Needham, G. B., Pamela's 218.
    daughters, N. Y., 1937.

Wicklein, E., Das 'Ernsthafte' in dem englischen 219.
    komischen roman des XVIII Jahrhunderts,
    Dresden, 1908.

XII. Some Important Early Publications

An essay on the new species of writing founded 220.
    by Mr. Fielding: with a word or two upon
    the modern state of criticism, London, 1751.

A catalogue of the entire and valuable library of 221.
    books of the late Henry Fielding, Esq.
    which will be sold at auction, London,
    [1755].
    Copy in British Museum with prices
    fetched in MS.

Lawrence, F., The life of Henry Fielding, with 222.
    notices of his writings, his times and his
    contemporaries, London, 1855.

Stephen, Leslie, ed., Works of Henry Fielding, 223.
    10v., London, 1882.

Aitken, G. A., "Henry Fielding" Athenaeum, 224.
    February 1, 1890.

VI.

A Bibliography of Thomas Frognall Dibdin
Author of the Bibliomania

Copyright 1950 by Francesco Cordasco

Contents

Introductory Note............................ 123

Part I: Works of Thomas Frognall Dibdin..... 125

Part II: Biographical and Critical Notices..... 131

Introductory Note

    The bibliographical works of Thomas Frognall Dibdin (1776-1847) have always been highly valued, and although his fame rests on that monumental catalogue which is the Bibliotheca Spenceriana, still, as the appended list shows, the work of Dibdin is varied and of considerable interest. There is hardly any doubt that his Bibliomania gave book collecting and bibliography a great impetus, and his Reminiscences of A Literary Life amply attests his interests and the importance of his associations. Even the irascible Henry G. Bohn, who exploited William T. Lowndes, did not dare break lances with Dibdin, and on every occasion referred to him as the "Rev. Dr. Dibdin".

    From the appearance of the Bibliotheca Spenceriana to the time of his death, Dibdin was the most important bibliographer in England. The reputation was deserved, and each year gave further notice of his powers. As early as 1812, Dibdin had achieved the foundation of the famous Roxburghe Club, and through the years he was largely responsible for its many accomplishments.

    It is hoped that our list will afford a guide to the collection of Dibdin, and, historically, allow his importance in the history of bibliography.

F. C.

Part I.
Works of Thomas Frognall Dibdin

For bibliography generally see William T. Lowndes, Bibliographer's Manual of English Literature, rev. H. G. Bohn
(6v. in 11v. London 1858-1864); Samuel A. Allibone, Critical Dictionary of English Literature and British and American Authors (1858-1871); Robert Watt, Bibliotheca Britannica (Edinburgh 4v. 1824).

1. An Introduction to the Knowledge of Rare and
   Valuable Editions of the Greek and Latin
   Classics. Gloucester 1802.
   Second edition: Introduction to the knowledge
   of the rare and valuable editions of the Greek
   and Latin classics, including the Scriptores
   de Re Rustica, Greek Romances, Lexicons
   and Grammars, with an account of Polyglot
   Bibles, the best editions of the Greek Septuagint
   and Testament. London 1804.
   Third edition: Ibid. with additional authors
   and biographical notices, chiefly of English
   editors. London 1808. 2v. Preface: "This
   edition does not contain the Index Analyticus
   of the last; nor the account of Latin editors
   of Greek writers--many references to catalogues and the specification of prices for which
   rare books have been sold, are also here sup-
   pressed."
   Fourth edition: Ibid. London 1827. 2v. This
   edition is completely rewritten. Lists for the
   first time an account of the best editions of
   the Hebrew bibles and of the Greek and Latin
   Fathers. Omits the Lexicography, Grammars
   and Collections, and Lists of Classics issued
   by various printers, given in the second and
   third editions. Only decoration is a facsimile
   plate of the Complutensian Polyglot given in the
   second and third edition.
   In this work, Dibdin was heavily indebted to
   the earlier labours of Dr. Edward Harwood
   whose A View of the various editions of the

Greek and Roman Classics, with remarks
had appeared in 1775, with later editions in
1778, 1782, 1790.

Bibliomania, or Book Madness. Containing some   2.
account of the history, symptoms, and cure
of this fatal disease. In an epistle addressed
to Richard Heber, Esq., being a supplement
to Dr. Ferriar's epistle on the same subject.
London 1809.
Second edition: Bibliomania or Book Madness:
A bibliographical romance in six parts.
London 1811. 2v.
Third edition: New edition with considerable
additions, including a key to the assumed
characters in the drama, and a supplement
edited by Dr. Dibdin himself. London, H. G.
Bohn 1842.
The second edition was reissued by The Bibliophile Society (4v., Boston 1903) with an introduction by R. Garnett and an essay on rare
books and their values by W. P. Cutter. A
key to the characters will be found in Bohn's
Lowndes.

The Bibliographical Decameron or Ten Days'   3.
Pleasant Discourse Upon Illuminated Manuscripts, and Subjects Connected with Early
Engraving, Typography, and Bibliography.
London 1817. 3v.
This work introduces the same characters of
the Bibliomania, and may be considered a
continuation of that work. Some copies have
a private plate of Mr. Thomas Payne, Bookseller, in spectacles. Bohn calls it "A model
of excellence and good taste in typography and
the arts".

Bibliotheca Spenceriana or A Descriptive Catalogue   4.
of the Books Printed in the Fifteenth Century, and of the Many Valuable First Editions
in the Library of George John Earl Spencer,
K. G. London 1814-15. 4v.
Only books printed in the Fifteenth century
and editiones principes. Fifty copies printed
with a portrait of Earl Spencer. The collection is now in the John Rylands Library in Manchester.

Thomas Frognall Dibdin

Aedes Althorpianae. To which is added a supplement to the Bibliotheca Spenceriana. London 1822. 2v.
Intended as a supplement to The Bibliotheca Spenceriana, forming vols. 5 and 6. Includes an account of the ancestors of Earl Spencer, a history of the mansion, with an account of the pictures and engravings in the gallery, a systematic catalogue of editions of the Scriptures, an account of the Aldine editions not contained in the former volumes. Includes an important supplement of books printed in the Fifteenth century.

5.

Catalogue of the Books Printed in the Fifteenth Century, Formerly in the Library of the Duke De Cassano Serra, and Now in Earl Spencer's Collection. London 1823.
This is the seventh volume of The Bibliotheca Spenceriana. It includes an index to the seven volumes. Lists many Fifteenth century items not in the other volumes.

6.

The Bibliographical, Antiquarian, and Picturesque Tour in France and Germany. London 1821. 3v.
Second edition: Ibid. London 1829. 3v.
This edition is abridged and omits all of the original plates excepting five, and adds seven new plates. See Bohn's Lowndes for a list of the plates of the first and second edition. Most of the copies which come up for sale are without the plates.
The first edition translated into French with notes by T. Licquet and G. A. Crapelet (Paris 1825. 4v.)

7.

Bibliographical, Antiquarian, and Picturesque Tour in the Northern Counties of England and of Scotland. London 1838. 2v.
An edition in the same year in imperial 8vo. (3v.) on large paper.

8.

The Library Companion or the Young Man's Guide and the Old Man's Comfort in the Choice of a Library. London 1824.
Second edition: Ibid. London 1825. With

9.

some corrections but omitting the Cracherode breeches story etc. Dibdin wrote a postscript which replied to criticism of the work. This postscript was separately published and is very rare.

10. <u>Sermons.</u> London 1820.
Sermons preached in King Street, Brompton, Quebec and Fitzroy Chapels.

11. <u>Sermons.</u> London 1825.
Sermons at St. Mary's Bryanston Square.

12. <u>The Sunday Library.</u> Being a Selection of Sermons from Eminent Divines of the Church of England Chiefly within the Last Half Century, with Biographical Sketches and notes. London 1831. 6v.

13. <u>Reminiscences of a Literary Life with Anecdotes of Books and Book-Collectors.</u> London 1836. 2v.
An index of 44 pages is often deficient. Includes many portraits and plates.

14. <u>The Quiz.</u>
A weekly journal edited in conjunction with Sir Robert Kerr Porter and his sisters. A fire consumed almost the whole of the impression, and it therefore is very rare. See the <u>Reminiscences.</u>

15. <u>Poems.</u> London 1797.
A great part of the impression destroyed. Very rare. See first edition of the <u>Bibliomania.</u>

16. <u>Chart of an Analysis of the Rights of Persons.</u> London 1798.
A large sheet, from a copper plate. Plate destroyed after printing 250.

17. <u>Specimen Bibliothecae Britannicae.</u> Specimen of a Digested Catalogue of Rare, Curious, and Useful Books in the English Language. London 1808.
Only 40 copies printed in 8vo., and 8 copies

Thomas Frognall Dibdin 129

(with woodcut) in 4to.

18. Specimen of an English De Bure. London 1810.
Only 16 leaves. Fifty copies printed.

19. Bibliography, A Poem. London 1812.
Pp. 24 consisting of 554 lines. Fifty copies printed.

20. The Lincoln Nosegay. [London 1811].
Eight leaves. Only 36 copies printed. Bohn's Lowndes notes that it was later surreptitiously printed.

21. Book Rarities or A Descriptive Catalogue of Some of the Most Curious, Rare and Valuable Books of Early Date. Chiefly in the Collection of George John, Earl Spencer, K. G. London 1811. Thirty-six copies printed.

22. Account of the First Printed Psalters at Mentz, in the Years 1457, 1459, and 1490. -- Observations on the Mentz Bible, Printed 1450-5.
Article on the Mentz bible appeared in Classical Review for 1811. The articles on the Psalter appeared in Aiken's Athenaeum, II, 376, 490. A few copies taken off separately.

23. Bibliophobia. Remarks on the Present Languid and Depressed State of Literature and the Book Trade in a Letter addressed to the Author of the Bibliomania by Mercurius Rusticus. London 1832.

24. La Belle Marianne. A Tale of Truth and Woe. London 1824.

25. Joseph Ames. Typographical Antiquities.
Being an Historical Account of Printing in England etc. A New Edition Greatly Enlarged with Copious Notes by T. F. Dibdin, D. D. London 1810-19. 4v. Ames's work had appeared in 1749. It had been considerably augmented by

William Herbert (1785-90. 3v.). Dibdin's edition was left unfinished. See [R. S. Maitland], An Index to Dibdin's Edition of the Typographical Antiquities..., London, Bibliographical Society 1899.

The Director. London 1807. 2v.   26.
A weekly literary journal. Dibdin wrote the bibliographical part.

Sir Thomas More's Utopia. A New Edition   27.
with Copious Notes and a Biographical and Literary Introduction. London 1808. 2v.
Rolinson's translation of 1551. Includes a portrait of More.

Thomas A. Kempis. Of the Imitation of Jesus   28.
Christ Translated from the Latin with an Introduction and Notes by the Rev. T. F. Dibdin, D.D. London 1828.
An elegant edition illustrated by six plates including the Salvator Mundi after Guercino. New edition in 1851 without introduction and plates.

Francis Quarles. Judgement and Mercy for   29.
Afflicted Souls or Meditations, Soliloquies and Prayers. New Edition with a Biographical and Critical Introduction. By Reginald Wolfe, Esq. London 1807.
Actually by Dibdin.

The History of Cheltenham and its Environs.   30.
Cheltenham 1803.

Fr. Fenelon. Treatise on the Education of   31.
Daughters Translated from the French and Adapted to English Readers with an Original Chapter on Religious Studies. By the Rev. T.F. Dibdin. Cheltenham 1805.

John Rastell. The Pastyme of People. The   32.
Cronycles of Dyuers Realmys and most Specyally of the Realm of England...

New Edition Now First Reprinted and
Systematically Arranged with Facsimile
Woodcuts. Edited by Rev. T. F. Dibdin,
D. D. London 1811.
Rastell's work had appeared in 1529.
Only 500 copies of Dibdin's edition printed.

Thomas Feylde. The Coplaynte of a Louers   33.
Lyfe. London: Wynkyn de Worde. n. d.
Dibdin did an edition in 1818 and presented
it to the Roxburghe Club.

Part II.
Biographical and Critical Notices

Haslewood, Roxburghe Revels. Edinburgh 1837.

Gentleman's Magazine, new series, XXIX
(January 1848), 87-92, 338.

Jerdan, Men I Have Known. London 1866.

Luard, "T. F. Dibdin," Dictionary of National
Biography.

W. E. A. Axon, "De Quincey and T. F. Dibdin,"
Library, 2nd series, VIII (1907), 267-274.

VII.

An Introduction to 18th Century
Medical Bibliography
With a Handlist of Medical References and
Bibliographies
Published in the 18th Century

Copyright 1950 by Francesco Cordasco

Contents

Introductory Note............................ 137

Part I: General References.................... 139

Part II: Medical References and Bibliographies. 141
Published in the 18th Century

Introductory Note

Eighteenth century medical research was versatile and enlightened. Every branch of the healing art knew a systematic investigation and labour, and in England, superintended by Scotch genius, Medicine realized great triumphs. William Cullen (1710-1790) was, perhaps, the most eminent of the many Edinburgh medical teachers and, like his Continental colleagues, his main concern was the foundation of a comprehensive system of Medicine. It has been claimed that the abstract speculation of Cullen and of the 18th century generally to found a truly universal system of medicine was doomed to failure and wasted the talents of its genius; still the accumulation of positive knowledge did not cease, and it was on the basis of these accurate observations that the next century was to pass on to its great advances. The theoretic tendency of the 18th century did not retard the gains of practical medicine; rather it enhanced and stimulated enquiry into objective science. Certainly, this is clear if one turns to the publications of the Century itself. It is in this interest that this chapter is offered. I have avoided modern bibliographies, and have chosen the literature of the 19th and 18th centuries, themselves, in the hope that the early guides would be most helpful. In Part I, I have listed 19th century biographical and bibliographical medical publications; in further illustration, Part II lists works of referential value published in the 18th century itself. The lists are not intended to be complete. They include only those works which I have used and found helpful in my reading of 18th century Medicine. The arrangement is alphabetical, and where the titles are not clear, some small annotation has been provided.

F. C.

Part I.
General References

Atkinson, J., Medical bibliography.   1.
   London 1834.

Annali della Medicina Fisiologico-pathologica.   2.
   5v. Milano 1824.

Baker, Sir George, Medical tracts read at the   3.
   College of Physicians between the years
   1767-1785. London 1818.

Bernstein, J. G., Bibliotheca medico-chirurgica.   4.
   Frankfort 1829.
   In German. A classified catalogue of works
   published in Europe between 1750-1828.

Bibliothèque Médicale, ou recueil periodique   5.
   d'extraits des melleurs ouvrages de
   médecine et de chirurgie. 78v. Paris
   1803-1823.

Biographia Medica Piemontese. 2v.   6.
   Torino 1824.

Biographie Médicale. 7v. Paris 1820-25.   7.

Briggs, James, An Index to the anatomical,   8.
   medical, chirurgical and physiological
   papers contained in the Transactions of
   the Royal Society of London, from the
   commencement of the work to the end
   of the year 1813. Chronologically and
   alphabetically arranged. Westminster 1814.

Brugnoli, G., A. Corradi, and C. Taruffi,   9.
   Bibliographia italiana delle scienze mediche.
   Bologna 1858.

A Catalogue of the library of the Royal College   10.
    of Surgeons in London. London 1831.
    Lists over 5,000 items, largely drawn
    from 18th century.

A Catalogue of the library of the Medical Society   11.
    of London. London 1803.
    Some 2,000 items, largely from 18th century.

Des Genettes, R. N. D., Essai de biographie et   12.
    de bibliographie médicale. Paris 1825.

Dictionnaire de médecine. 21v. Paris 1821-28.   13.
    Many bibliographical notes.

Dictionnaire des sciences médicales, par une   14.
    société des médecins et chirurgiens. 60v.
    Paris 1812-22.

Nouvelle bibliothèque médicale augmentée d'un   15.
    recueil de médicine veterinaire. 17v.
    1823-1827.

Ploucquet, W. G., Literatura medica digesta   16.
    sive repertorium medicinae practicae
    chirurgiae, atque rei obstetriciae. 4v.
    Tubungae 1808-1809.
    A monumental catalogue, bibliographical
    and critical.

Précis de l'histoire de la médecine et de la   17.
    bibliographie médicale. Paris 1826.

Roy, C. H., Catalogus bibliothecae medicae.   18.
    Amsterdam 1830.
    A systematic catalogue of works in
    European languages on all branches of
    Medicine.

Royston, William, Observations on the rise and   19.
    progress of the medical art in the British
    Empire; containing remarks on medical
    literature and a view of bibliographical
    medicine. London 1818.

Watt, Robert, A Catalogue of medical books for   20.
    the use of students attending lectures on

the principles and practice of medicine.
With an address to medical students on
the best method of prosecuting their studies.
Glasgow 1812.
Reprinted with introduction by F. Cordasco,
New York, 1950.
Lists over 1,000 items.

Watt, Robert, Bibliotheca Britannica. 4v. 21.
Edinburgh 1824.
Important notices for medical bibliography.

Part II.
Medical References and Bibliographies
Published in the 18th Century

Baldinger, E. G., Sylloge selectiorum 22.
opusculorum argumenti medico practici.
Göttingen 1776-1782.

Baldinger, E. G., Opuscula medica. Göttingen 23.
1787.
A continuation of No. 22. Like No. 22,
largely unannotated.

Baldinger, E. G., Litteratura universa materiae 24.
medicae, alimentariae, toxicologiae,
pharmaciae et therapiae generalis medicae
atque chirurgicae pottissimum academica.
Marburg 1793.
A truly universal catalogue. Descriptive
and critical.

[Sir Joseph Banks] Catalogus bibliothecae 25.
historico-naturalis Josephi Banks, Baroneti,
auctore Jo. Dryander. 5v. London 1798-
1800.
One of the great medical collections of the
century.

Beer, G. J., Bibliotheca ophthalmica. Re- 26.
pertorium aller bis zu Ende des Jahrs
1797, erschienenen Schriften über die
augenkrankheiten. 3v. Wien 1799.
An important specialized catalogue.

Black, William, An historical sketch of medicine 27.
and surgery from their origin to the present
time. London 1782.
Many bibliographical notes.

Bibliotheca anatomico-medico-chirurgica. 3v. 28.
London 1711-14.
An important, unannotated catalogue for
early items.

Bibliothecae collegii regalis medicorum 29.
Londoniensis catalogus. London 1757.

Carrere, Joseph F., Bibliothèque litteraire, 30.
historique et critique de la médicine
ancienne et moderne, contenant l'histoire
des médecins, chirurgiens, anatomistes...
2v. Paris 1776.

A Catalogue of the library of Dr. F. Bernard. 31.
London 1764.
An important anatomical collection.

Commentarii de rebus in scientia naturali et 32.
medicina gestis, cum supplementis quatuor,
et tribus voluminibus indicis. 44v.
Leipzig 1752-93.
A compendious history, bibliographical and
critical.

Douglas, J., Bibliographia anatomica sive 33.
catalogus omnium penè auctorum qui ab
Hippocrate ad Harvaeum rem anatomicam
ex professo, vel obiter, scriptis illustrarunt.
Lugd. Bat. 1734.
Many references to 18th century anatomical
study.

Goulin, Jena, Mémoires littéraires, critiques, 34.
physiologiques, biographiques et biblio-
graphiques pour servir à l'histoire ancienne et moderne de la médicine. Paris
1777.
A systematic introduction to the literature
of the history of Medicine.

18th Century Medical Bibliography   143

35. Hill, John, A Review of the works of the Royal Society of London, containing animadversions on such of the papers as deserve particular observation. London 1780.

36. Hutchinson, B., Biographica medica, or memoirs of eminent medical characters from the earliest account to the present period, with a catalogue of their works. London 1799.
Invaluable for 18th century English physicians.

37. James, Robert, A Medical Dictionary. 3v. London 1743-45.
Excellent digest of Medicine at the mid-century.

38. Saggi scientifici e letterarii dell' accademia di Padova. Padova 1786-1794.
Guide to the work of the foremost medical center of 18th century Italy.

VIII.

The 18th Century Novel
A Handlist of General Histories and Articles of the Last Twenty-five Years with a Notice of Bibliographical Guides

Copyright 1950 by Francesco Cordasco

Contents

Preface.. 149

Introductory Note by Professor James R. Foster. 151

Part   I: General Bibliographical Guides......... 153

Part II: General Histories and Articles of the
            Last Twenty-five Years............... 155

Part III: Important French Literary History..... 164

Subject Index................................... 165

Preface

In no field of literary investigation, perhaps, has the scholarship of the last quarter century been so successful as in that of 18th century prose fiction. The major novelists have been studied with candour and enthusiasm, and the origins of their fiction have been discerned in native tradition and foreign impression. The extent of this interest and its fecundity are indicated in the antecedent numbers of this bibliographical series, where, upwards of five hundred titles on the major novelists have been assembled. This compilation proposes the listing of all general histories and general articles dealing with 18th century prose fiction which have appeared in the last twenty-five years.

In the matter of arrangement, I have preferred alphabetical notice by authors, but a subject-index has been given to facilitate reference. Annotation is restricted to notices of important reviews or brief titular elucidation. The reader is advised to consult further the Annual bibliography of English language and literature (Modern Humanities Research Association, 1920-date); Year's work in English Studies (English Association, 1921-date); English literature, 1660-1800: A current bibliography (Philological Quarterly, 1926-date).

Professor James R. Foster, who has been an important part of the novel scholarship of these years, and whose History of The Pre-Romantic Novel in England will long remain a testimony to meticulous scholarship, has provided an introductory note which briefly reviews the contribution of the quarter-century.

F. C.

Introductory Note

Within memory, the attitude toward 18th century prose fiction largely directed itself to an appreciation of the great novelists of the period. The best seller of the century, and the novel of the circulating library, both graphic commentaries on the tastes and predilections of the age, were considered unimportant for university study. Where admitted in the university seminar, the minor novel suffered depreciation, and the haughty aloofness of a critic like George Saintsbury, who considered all of Prévost's novels, except Manon Lescaut, as worthless, is indicative of the general temper. The Pre-romantic fiction remained in the academic shadow of the Fielding-Smollett tradition which alone was admitted to the importance of the dissertation and critique.

However, the last twenty-five years have corrected this unfortunate emphasis. Students have turned to the minor novel, and their studies have importantly modified the many misconceptions of origin and motive even in the prose giants of the period. It was appropriate that this study should have begun in France, for here, in the minor fiction lay many of the seeds of emotion and extravagant sentiment which were to be carried across the Channel. Distinguished in this early French scholarship was the work of Etienne (Le Genre Romanesque) who studied seriously and in much detail the minor novels of the century in France. Etienne showed that the usual estimation of Rousseau's influence was in error, and, most significantly, that Richardson's total impression on the fiction of the century had known much erroneous emphasis. Fairchild's Noble Savage directed attention to the ideological importance of many minor 18th century novels, especially those with primitivistic themes. Gray's unpublished Harvard dissertation (The Fielding-Smollett Tradition) seriously modified the traditional views. It had become evident that, excepting the imitators of Sterne, the vein of origin, motive, model for the widely-read minor novel still remained unexplored. The necessity of this examination was apparent by the need for a more searching study of the great novelists and their connections with the minor fiction. In many instances the minor fiction held the key to the giants' origins and model.

Generally, the last quarter-century has shown the student of the novel equal to the arduous task of new exploration and evaluation. Much, however, still remains to be done. There is no satisfactory bibliography of 18th century fiction. Clapp's labors never knew publication, and, alas!, who will attempt them? Of all the major novelists Smollett deserves more penetrating study, and behind him are the Spanish novels of the 17th century whose apparent influence on the satirico-picaresque _genre_ has known little study.

Professor Cordasco's handlist of the studies of the last twenty-five years will admirably furnish not only an introduction to the novel, but to that research which must be extended and completed. Here is assembled the scholarship, and here is indicated its problem and solution.

James R. Foster

Part I.
General Bibliographical Guides

1. Ernest A. Baker, A Guide to the best fiction in English. London 1913. Revised, J. Peckham, London 1932.

2. _____, History of the English novel 10v., London 1924-39.

3. Ernest Bernbaum, "Recent works on prose fiction before 1800," Modern Language Notes, XLII (1927), 281-93.
   Irregularly appears in Ibid. thereafter.

4. Andrew Block, The English novel, 1740-1850. A catalogue including prose romances, short stories and translations of foreign works. London 1939.

5. Cambridge bibliography of English literature, 4v. Cambridge 1941. II, 488-566.

6. John M. Clapp, "A bibliography of English fiction in the Eighteenth Century," Papers of the Bibliographical Society of America, VI (1911), 37-56.
   Outlines for a list of English prose fiction. Never completed.

7. Francesco Cordasco, Eighteenth Century Bibliographical Pamphlets. Long Island University Press 1947--.
   The first five numbers collect criticism of Richardson, Fielding, Smollett and Sterne.

8. _____, A Register of 18th Century bibliographies and references. A Chronological quarter-century survey..... Chicago 1950.

9. A. Esdaile, A List of English tales and prose romances printed before 1740. London 1912.

Eighteenth Century Bibliographies

A remarkable collection of books illustrating 10.
the history of the English novel, tale,
and prose romance. On sale by C. A.
Stonehill, jr. London 1937. Catalogue
No. 134.
Deposited in Hunter College Library,
New York City.

James E. Tobin, Eighteenth Century English 11.
literature and its cultural background.
A bibliography. New York, Fordham
University Press 1939.

Further Bibliographical Information

In addition to the formal lists enumerated above, valuable bibliographical information may be sought in the older histories: Raleigh, The English Novel (1896); Cross, Development of the English Novel (1899) and Dunlop, History of Prose Fiction (rev. Wilson, 1906). For the study of particular types, the following are of aid: Conant, Oriental Tale in England (1908); Morgan, Rise of the Novel of Manners (1911); Chandler, The Literature of Roguery (1907).

For general information, the verification of titles or the comprehensive notice of titles, the most valuable single source remains the British Museum Catalogue. But it must be supplemented by consultation of the 18th century magazines (Gentlemen's Magazine; Monthly Review etc.); Arber's reprint of the Term Catalogues of the London booksellers from 1701-1711; The Dictionary of National Biography; Upcott's Biographical Dictionary of Living Authors (1816); Notes & Queries; The Harvard Catalogue of Chap-books and Broadside Ballads (1905); Brydges's Censura Literaria (1815), and Restituta (1814-16); Hazlitt's Handbook to the Literature of Great Britain (1867); Lowndes's Bibliographer's Manual (rev. Bohn, 1858-64); Watt, Bibliotheca Britannica (4v. 1824); and the Catalogue of the Advocates' Library at Edinburgh (1867-79).

In the matter of French influence on the English novel of the 18th century profitable use may be made of the contemporary L'Usage des Romans by Lenglet-Dufresnoy (1734); Bibliothèque Universelle des Romans (1775-1805); Catalogue LeValliere (1783). Invaluable are Quérard's La France Littéraire (1827-64) and Gay's Bibliographie des Ouvrages relatifs a L'Amour (1893). See also Alexandre N. Pigoreau, Petite Bibliographie Biographico-Romancière (1821).

Part II.
General Histories and Articles of the Last Twenty-Five Years

12. Robert A. Aubin, "Some Augustan Gothicists," Harvard Studies and notes in Philology and Literature, XVII (1935), 15-26.

13. Philip G. Babcock, The imaginary voyage in prose fiction: a history of its criticism and a guide to its study, with an annotated check list of 215 imaginary voyages from 1700-1800. New York, Columbia University Press 1941.

14. Ernest A. Baker, The history of the English novel. Vol. III: The later romances and the establishment of realism; Vol. IV: Intellectual realism from Richardson to Sterne; Vol. V: The novel of Sentiment and the Gothic romance. London 1929-34.

15. Frank Gees Black, "The continuators of Pamela," Revue Anglo-Américaine, XIII (1936).

16. _____, "The English epistolary novel from 1740 to 1800," Harvard University Summaries of Theses, 1936. 1938, pp. 307-10.

17. _____, The epistolary novel in the late 18th century. A descriptive and bibliographical study. (University of Oregon Monographs. Studies in Literature and philology, No. 2). Eugene, University of Oregon 1940. Appendix A lists 816 items of epistolary fiction, 1740-1840.

18. Edith Birkhead, "Sentiment and sensibility in the 18th century English novel," Essays and Studies, XI (1925), 92-116.

19. Johanna Birnbaum, Die "Memoirs" um 1700: Eine Studie zur Entwicklung der realistischen Romankunst vor Richardson. Halle 1934.

Benjamin Bissell, The American Indian in 20.
  English literature of the 18th Century.
  New Haven, Yale University Press, 1925.

Edmund Blunden, Votive tables: studies chiefly 21.
  appreciative of English authors and books.
  London 1931.
  Essays on Bunyan, Defoe, Steele, Goldsmith, Churchill etc.

Jacob Brauchli, Der englische Schauerroman um 22.
  1800 unter Berücksichitigung der unbekannten
  Bücher: ein Beitrag zur Geschichte der
  Volksliteratur. Weida i. Thür: Thomas &
  Hubert 1928.
  Lists some 300 "Novels of terror," See
  Philological Quarterly, VIII (1929), 172-73.

H. R. Brown, The Sentimental novel in 23.
  America, 1789-1860. Durham, North
  Carolina 1940.

Wallace Cable Brown, "Prose fiction and English 24.
  interest in the Near East, 1775-1825,"
  Publications of the Modern Language
  Association, LIII (1938), 827-36.

Gerhard Buck, Die Vorgeschichte des historischen 25.
  Romans in der modernen englischen
  literatur. Hamburg 1931.
  Reviewed by S. B. Liljegren, Beiblatt,
  XLIII (1932), 169-72.

Kenneth Clark, The Gothic revival, New 26.
  York 1928.
  Important non-literary materials for the
  genre.

R. S. Crane, "Suggestions toward a genealogy 27.
  of the 'Man of Feeling'," ELH: A Journal
  of English Literary History, I (1934),
  205-230.

Andrew L. Drummon, "English nonconformity in 28.
  fiction," London Quarterly And Holborn
  Review, CLXIX (1944), 310-25.

29. Thomas C. D. Eaves, "Graphic illustration of the principal English novels of the 18th century," Harvard University... summaries of theses... 1943-45. Cambridge, 1947, pp. 469-71.

30. Claire-Eliane Engel, "Autour du voyage de l'abbé Prévost en Angleterre," Revue de Littérature Comparée. XVIII (1938), 506-10.

31. _____, Figures et aventures du XVIIIe siècle, Voyages et découvertes de l'abbé Prévost. (Etudes de littérture, d'art et d'histoire 5) Paris 1939.

32. _____, "English novels in Switzerland in the XVIIIth century," Comparative Literature Studies, XIV & XV (1944), 2-8.

33. Henry C. Fisher, "Realism and morality in English fiction before 1750," University of Pittsburgh Bulletin: Abstracts of theses, XIV (1938), 79-85.

34. James R. Foster, "The Abbé Prévost and the English novel," Publications of the Modern Language Association, XLII (1927), 443-64.

35. _____, "The Minor English novelists, 1750-1800," Harvard University Summaries of theses, II (1930), 172-75.

36. _____, The History of the pre-romantic novel in England. Modern Language Association 1949.
"The aim of this book is to give an account of the pre-romantic narratives which appeared in England during the eighteenth century and to describe the French novels influencing them." (Preface)

37. W. F. Gallaway, "The Conservative attitude toward fiction, 1770-1830," Publications of the Modern Language Association, LV (1940), 1041-59.

Edward L. Giles, "Shipwrecks and desert islands," Notes & Queries, CLXXVII (1939), 218-20.   38.

Ernest W. Gray, The Fielding-Smollett tradition in the English novel from 1750-1835. Unpublished Harvard University dissertaion. 1931.   39.

Ursula Habel, Die Nachwirkung des picaresken Romans in England (von Nash bis Fielding und Smollett). Breslau 1930.   40.

T. P. Haviland, The Roman de Longue Haleine on English soil. Philadelphia 1931.   41.

Joseph B. Heidler, The history, from 1700 to 1800, of English criticism of prose fiction. (University of Illinois Studies in Language and Literature XIII, no. 2) Urbana 1928.   42.

Robert B. Heilman, "The English novel, 1760-1800, and the American Revolution," Harvard University summaries of theses, 1935. 1937, pp. 271-74.   43.

_____, America in English fiction, 1760-1800. The Influences of the American Revolution. (Louisiana State University Studies no. 33) Baton Rouge 1937.   44.

Katherine G. Hornbeak, The Complete letter writer in English, 1568-1800. (Smith College Studies... Vol. XV, nos. 3-4) Northampton, Smith College 1934.   45.

Joyce M. Horner, The English women novelists and their connection with the feminist movement (1688-1797). (Smith College Studies... Vol. XI, nos. 1-3) Northampton, Smith College 1929-30.   46.

Susanne Howe, Wilhelm Meister and his English kinsmen, New York 1930.   47.

The 18th Century Novel

48. Helen Sard Hughes, "The middle-class reader and the English novel," *Journal of English and Germanic Philology*, XXV (1926), 362-78.

49. R. M. Lovett and H. S. Hughes, *History of the novel in England.* Boston 1932.

50. Q. D. Leavis, *Fiction and the reading public.* London 1932.

51. B. G. MacCarthy, *Women writers: their contribution to the English novel, 1621-1744.* Cork, Cork University Press 1945.

52. _____, *The later women novelists, 1744-1818.* Cork University Press; Oxford, Basil Blackwell 1948.

53. Sir John Marriott, *English history in English fiction.* London 1940.

54. Robert D. Mayo, "The Gothic short story in the magazines," *Modern Language Review*, XXXVII (1942), 448-54.

55. _____, "How long was Gothic fiction in vogue?", *Modern Language Notes*, LVIII (1943), 56-64.
 A study of the *Lady's Magazine* as representative of popular taste.

56. John McClelland, "The course of realism in the English novel from Addison and Steele through Sir Walter Scott," *Abstracts of Dissertations*, Stanford University, 1933-34, pp. 52-54.

57. Bruce McCullough, *Representative English novelists: Defoe to Conrad.* New York 1946.
 "My purpose... is not to trace the history of the English novel... but to subject a limited number of representative novels to a more searching scrutiny than would be possible in a general survey."

K. K. Mehrotra, Horace Walpole and the 58.
English novel, 1764-1820. Oxford 1934.

C. M. Newlin, "The English periodicals and the 59.
novel, 1709-40," Michigan Academy of
Science Papers, XVI (1931).

Marjorie Hope Nicholson, "Cosmic voyages," 60.
ELH: A Journal of English Literary
History, VII (1940), 83-107.

_____, Voyages to the moon. New York 1948. 61.

Coleman O. Parsons, "The progenitors of Black 62.
Beauty in humanitarian literature," Notes
& Queries, CXCII (1947), 156-58, 190-03,
210-13, 230-32.

Edgar Pelham, The Art of the novel: from 1700 63.
to the present time. London 1934.

E. Pons, "Le 'voyage' genre littéraire au XVIIIe 64.
siècle," Bulletin de la Faculté des lettres
de Strasbourg, IV (1926), 97-101, 144-49,
201-07.
Useful outlines and bibliographies.

J. Prinsen, De roman in de 18e eeuw in West- 65.
Europa. Groningen 1925.
Reviewed in Philological Quarterly, V
(1926), 351.

C. B. A. Proper, Social elements in English 66.
prose fiction between 1700 and 1832.
Amsterdam 1929.

Eino Railo, The Haunted Castle: a study of the 67.
elements of English Romanticism. London
1927.

Paul Lambert Richards, "The Italian novel as in- 68.
fluenced by English Gothic fiction, 1820-
40," Harvard University...summaries of
theses..., 1939. 1942, pp. 277-80.

Sir Herbert Richmond, "The naval officer in 69.
fiction," Essays and Studies by Members

of the English Association, XXX (1944), 7-25.

70. W. Roberts, "A shelf of 18th century novels," Book Collectors' Quarterly, July 1934.

71. Winifred H. Rogers, "The reaction against melodramatic sentimentality in the English novel, 1796-1830," Publications of the Modern Language Association, XLIX (1934), 98-122.

72. Helen Cooke Sarchet, "Women in English fiction of the mid-eighteenth century, from 1740-1771," Summaries of Ph. D. theses, University of Minnesota, II (1943), 146-49.

73. Charlotte Schlötke, "Entwicklungsstufen des humoristisch-satyrischen Romans in England und Frankreich: Rabelais-Swift-Sterne," Geist der Zeit, XVI (1938), 166-75.

74. Walter S. Scott, The Bluestocking ladies. London 1947.
Notices of Mary Delany, Elizabeth Carter, etc.

75. Archibald B. Shepperson, The Novel in motley. A history of the burlesque novel in English. Cambridge, Harvard University Press 1936. Reviewed by J. W. Beach, Journal of English and Germanic Philology, XXXVI (1937), 440-442. See Philological Quarterly, XVII (1938), 181.

76. Godfrey F. Singer, The epistolary novel. University of Pennsylvania Press 1933.

77. Kenneth Chester Slagle, The English country squire as depicted in English prose fiction from 1740-1800. University of Pennsylvania 1938.

78. W. H. Smith, Architecture in English fiction, New Haven 1934.

79. Morris Edmund Speare, The Political novel: its development in England and in America. New York, Oxford University Press 1924.

H. W. Streeter, The 18th century English novel in French translation. A bibliographical study. New York 1936.
See additions, Modern Philology, XXXV (1938), 457-61. — 80.

Cony Sturgis, The Spanish world in English fiction. A bibliography. Boston 1927. — 81.

Montague Summers, "The Illustrations of the 'Gothick' novels," Connoisseur, XCII (1936), 266-71. — 82.

———, The Gothic quest. A history of the Gothic novel. London, Fortune Press [1938]. Reprinted Columbia University Press 1941. — 83.

———, A Gothic bibliography. London, Fortune Press [1940]. — 84.

Feltus Wylie Sypher, "The anti-slavery movement to 1800 in English Literature, exclusive of the periodical," Harvard University summaries of theses, 1937. 1938. — 85.

Sister Mary Muriel Tarr, Catholicism in Gothic fiction: a study of the nature and function of Catholic materials in Gothic fiction in England (1762-1820). Washington, Catholic University of America 1946. — 86.

Houghton W. Taylor, "Modern fiction and the doctrine of uniformity," Philological Quarterly, XIX (1940), 225-36. — 87.

John Tinnon Taylor, Early opposition to the English novel: the popular reaction from 1780-1830. Columbia University, King's Crown Press 1943. — 88.

P. Van Tieghem, "La sensibilité et la passion dans la roman européen au xviiie siècle," Revue de Littérature Comparée, VI (1926), 424-35. — 89.

The 18th Century Novel

90. J. W. S. Tompkins, The popular novel in England, 1770-1800. London 1932.
Reviewed G. Greene, Spectator, August 20, 1932, pp. 238-39.

91. Wilmer Kohl Trauger, "Pedagogues and pupils: a study in 18th century fiction," Harvard University... summaries of theses, 1940. 1942, pp. 373-78.

92. R. P. Utter and G. B. Needham, Pamela's daughters. New York 1936.
18th and 19th century heroines as exemplars of delicacy and virtue.

93. H. R. S. Van der Veen, Jewish characters in 18th century English fiction and drama. Groningen 1935.

94. Edward Wagenknecht, Cavalcade of the English novel. New York [1943].

95. J. H. Warner, "18th century English reactions to the Nouvelle Héloise," Publications of the Modern Language Association, LII (1937).

96. Harold Francis Watson, The Sailor in English fiction and drama, 1550-1800. New York, Columbia University Press 1931.
Reviewed in Philological Quarterly, XI (1932), 182.

97. W. W. Watt, Shilling shockers of the Gothic school. Cambridge, Harvard University Press 1932.

98. Lois Whitney, Primitivism and the idea of progress in English popular literature of the 18th century. Baltimore 1934.

99. Roy McKeen Wiles, "Prose fiction in English periodical publications before 1750," Harvard University summaries of theses, 1935. 1937, pp. 289-92.

Elisabeth Binz Winiger, Erziehungsfragen in 100.
den Romanen von Samuel Richardson,
Henry Fielding, Tobias Smollett, Oliver
Goldsmith, Laurence Sterne. Zürich 1926.

Mary W. Winspear, "The English 'Man of 101.
Feeling': changing ethical and social
values as revealed in the 18th century
novel," University of Toronto Disseration
Abstracts for 1943.

Walter F. Wright, Sensibility in English prose 102.
fiction, 1760-1814: a reinterpretation.
(Illinois Studies in Language and Literature,
Vol. XXII, nos. 3-4) Urbana, 1937.

Hildegard Zeller, Die Ich-erzählung in englischen 103.
roman. Breslan 1933.

Part III.
Important French Literary History

Edmond Estève, Etudes de la littérature 104.
préromantique. Paris 1920.

Servais Etienne Le Genre Romanesque en France 105.
depuis l'apparition de la 'Nouvelle Héloise"
jusqu-aux approches de la Révolution.
Paris 1922.

Paul Hazard, Quatres Etudes, New York 1940. 106.
One study is on the Man of Feeling.

A. Monglond, Histoire intérieure du préromantisme 107.
français. Grenoble 1929. 2v.

Louis Reynaud, Le Romantisme: Ses origines 108.
Anglo-Germaniques. Paris 1926.

Pierre Trahard, Les maitres de la sensibilité 109.
française au XVIIIe siècle, 1715-1789.
Paris 1931. 4v.

Paul Van Tieghem, Le Préromantisme. Paris 110.
1924-30. 2v.

Subject Index
References are to bibliographical entry numbers

American Indian, 20
American Revolution, 43, 44
Anti-Slavery movement, 85
Architecture, 78

Black Beauty, 62
Bluestocking ladies, 74
Burlesque novel, 75

East, the, 24
Epistolary novel, 76

Feminist movement, 46
Fielding-Smollett tradition, 39
French translations, 80

Gothic novel, 12, 22, 26, 54, 55, 67, 82, 83, 84, 86, 97

Historical novel, 25
History, 53

Illustrations, 29
Imaginary voyage, 13, 60, 61, 64
Italian novel, 68

Jewish characters, 93

Letter writer, 45

Man of Feeling, 27, 101, 106
Memoirs, 19
Middle-class reader, 48
Minor novelists, 35

Naval officer, 69
Nonconformity, 28
Nouvelle Héloise, 95, 105

Pamela, 15, 92
Pedagogical novel, 91

Periodicals, 59, 99
Political novel, 79
Popular novel, 90
Pre-romantic novel, 36, 104, 110
Primitivism, 98
Prévost, Abbé, 30, 31, 34, 36

Reading public, 50
Realism, 56

Sailor, 96
Satirical novel, 73
Sensibility, 18, 23, 27, 89, 102
Sentimentalism, 18, 23, 27, 36, 71
Social elements, 66
Spain, 81
Squire, 77
Switzerland, 32

Horace Walpole, 58
Wilhelm Meister, 47
Women in fiction, 72
Women novelists, 46, 51, 52

IX.

William Godwin
A Handlist of Critical Notices & Studies

Copyright 1950 by Francesco Cordasco

Note

With the publication of Priestley's edition of Godwin's Political Justice a great stimulus will be given to the study, afresh, of its influence and great impression. William Godwin was the political mentor of many of the Romantics, and if, as for Shelley, his influence was to be mixed with despair and the flight to Platonic unreality, still the Godwinian lodestar is unmistakable, clear, inescapable. Godwin epitomises the French Encyclopaedic Revolt, and through his mind the French philosophe makes his entry into the English scene. Holbach, Helvetius, Condorcet, Rousseau, all are distilled in the pages of the Political Justice and the residue held fascination and hope for the English thinker. As English Romanticism is rooted in the doctrines of the 18th century philosophic enlightenment, so William Godwin is the introduction to its comprehension.

We have collected, herein, the major criticism of William Godwin. Some bibliographical notes have been added. The arrangement is alphabetical, and for certain items reviews have been cited.

F. C.

I. Note on Godwin Bibliography

For general bibliography see Cambridge Bibliography of English Literature, II, 655-56. A full list of Godwin's writings is in F. K. Brown, William Godwin (see infra). For editions of the Political Justice see Priestley's edition, infra, which discusses the 1st, 2nd, 3rd editions and contains bibliographical notes.

II. Critical Notices and Studies

1. M. Ray Adams, "Mary Hays, disciple of William Godwin," Publications of Modern Language Association of America, LV (1940), 472-83.

2. A. O. Aldridge, "Jonathan Edwards and William Godwin on virtue," American Literature, XVIII (1947), 308-18.

3. B. S. Allen, "Reaction against William Godwin," Modern Philology, XVI (1918).

4. _____, "William Godwin and the Stage," Publications of the Modern Language Association of America, XXXV (1920).

5. _____, "Godwin's influence upon John Thelwall," Publications of the Modern Language Association of America XXXVII (1922).

6. H. N. Brailsford, Shelley, Godwin and their Circle. London 1913.

7. Ford K. Brown, Life of William Godwin. London and New York 1926.
Rev. W. R. Dennes, University of Calif. Chronicle, XXVIII (1926), 460-62.

8. Floyd H. Deen, "The genesis of Martin Faber in Caleb Williams," Modern Language Notes, LIX (1944), 315-17.

171

O. Earle, "The reputation and influence of 9.
    William Godwin in America," Harvard
    University summaries of theses 1938
    (1940), pp. 289-94.

D. Fleisher, "William Godwin: his background, 10.
    thought and influence on Shelley's forma-
    tive period," Harvard University...
    summaries of theses...1941 (1945),
    pp. 335-38.

R. Gourg, William Godwin, sa vie, ses 11.
    oeuvres principales. Paris 1908.

William Hazlitt, "William Godwin" in The 12.
    Spirit of the Age (1825). Rep. in
    Works, ed. Waller and Glover, IV (1902).

_____, "Mr. Godwin," Edinburgh Review, 13.
    April, 1830. Rep. Works, ed. cit., X
    (1904).

A. Koszuel and G. Bresch, "Un lettre de 14.
    William Godwin," Revue Anglo-
    Américaine, VI (1929), 430-32.
    To Thomas Holcroft, October 10, 1819.

W. M. Merchant, "Wordsworth's Godwinian 15.
    period," Comparative Literature
    Studies, IV (1942), 18-23.

J. Meyer, William Godwins Romane. Ein 16.
    Beitrag zur Geschichte des englischen
    Romans. Leipzig 1906.

F. Norman, "A Godwin Pamphlet," [London] 17.
    Times Literary Supplement, July 28,
    1942, p. 367.
    Describes "Letters of Verax to the
    Editor of the 'London Chronicle' 1815."

C. Kegan Paul, William Godwin, his friends 18.
    and contemporaries. London 1876. 2v.

Raymond A. Preston, ed., An Enquiry concerning 19.
    Political Justice and its influence on general

virtue and happiness.
New York 1926. 2v.
Reprint of 1st edition (1793) with omission
of 11 chapters.

20. F. E. L. Priestley, "Platonism in William
Godwin's Political Justice," Modern
Language Quarterly, IV (1943), 63-69.

21. F. E. L. Priestley, ed., An Enquiry concerning
Political Justice and its influence on general virtue and happiness. A photographic
facsimile of the 3rd edition. Corrected and
edited with variant readings of the 1st and
2nd eds. and with a critical introduction and
notes. University of Toronto Press 1947. 3v.
Rev. F. M. Watkins, Canadian Journal of
Economics and Political Science, XIV, 107-
112.

22. P. Ramus, William Godwin der Theoretiker des
kommunistischen Anarchismus. Eine
biographische Studie mit Auszügen aus
seiner Schriften. Leipzig 1907.

23. H. Roussin, William Godwin. Paris 1913.

24. H. Saitzeff, William Godwin und die Anfänge
des Anarchismus im XVIII. Jahrhundert.
Berlin 1907.

25. H. Simon, William Godwin and Mary
Wollstonecroft. Munich 1909.

26. Leslie Stephen, "William Godwin's Novels"
in Studies of a Biographer, III (1902).

27. E. Stone, "Caleb Williams and Martin Faber:
a contrast," Modern Language Notes,
LXII (1947), 480-83.

28. M. S. Storr, "L'Amour et le marriage chez
Godwin," Revue Anglo-Américaine, X
(1932), 31-45.

29. "William Godwin: apostle of universal benevolence," [London] Times Literary Supplement, April 4, 1936, 285-6.

30. George Woodcock, William Godwin: a biographical study with a foreword by Herbert Read. London 1946.

X.

Edward Gibbon
A Handlist of Critical Notices & Studies

Copyright 1950 by Francesco Cordasco

Part I.
General Bibliography

J. E. Norton, A bibliography of the works of Edward Gibbon. London 1940. Rev. D. M. Low, Review of English Studies, XVII (1940), 361-63.   1.

D. M. Low, "Edward Gibbon," Cambridge Bibliography of English Literature, Cambridge 1941 3v., II, pp. 882-885.   2.

The Library of Edward Gibbon. A catalogue of his books. With an introduction by Geoffrey Keynes. London 1940. Rev. J. E. N., Library, 4th series, XXI (1940), 218-23. See No. 30.   3.

Le Journal de Gibbon à Lausanne, 17 Aout 1763--19 Avril 1764. Publié par Georges Bonnard. Lausanne: Librarie de l'université 1945.   4.

Gibbon's journal to January 28, 1763. My Journal, I, II, III, and Ephemerides. With introductory essays by D. M. Low. London 1929.
For editions and bibliographical problems of The Decline and Fall see J. B. Bury's edition (7v., 1909-14) which contains bibliography by H. M. Beatty, VII, pp. 348-64. For corrections to text see [London] Times Literary Supplement, July 24, 31, 1924 and revised text, 7v., 1926-9.   5.

Part II.
Biography and General Criticism

T. P. Armstrong, "Gibbon and St. George," Notes & Queries, CLXXV (1938), 209-10.   6.

F. Baldensperger, "A neglected letter of 7.
   Edward Gibbon (Lausanne 1792),"
   Modern Language Forum, XXVII (1942),
   111-14.
   A letter to the antiquary John Nichols.

W. Barry, "Gibbon," Quarterly Review, 8.
   January (1897).
   Continued, ibid., January (1898).

A. Beaunier, "Trois amis de Mme. de Stael," 9.
   Revue des Deux Mondes, February (1917).

C. F. Bell, "The iconography of Edward Gibbon," 10.
   [London] Times Literary Supplement,
   June 21, 1929, p. 494.
   See comment, ibid., July 25, 1929;
   August 1, 1929.

J. B. Black, The Art of History. A Study of 11.
   four great historians of the 18th Century.
   London 1926.

E. Blunden, Edward Gibbon and his Age. 12.
   Bristol 1935.

Georges Bonnard, "L'importance du deuxième 13.
   sèjour de Gibbon à Lausanne dans la
   formation de l'historien" in Mélanges
   d' histoire et de littérature offerts à
   Monsieur Charles Gilliard, Lausanne 1944,
   pp. 400-20.

Emile Boulan, "Madame Necker, 1737-1794," 14.
   Neophilologus, XXXI (1947), 84-89.

T. C. C._____, "A reading in Gibbon," Notes & 15.
   Queries, CLXXXIII (1942), 328.

R. W. Chapman, "A reading in Gibbon," 16.
   Notes & Queries, CLXXXIII (1942), 255.

E. Clodd, Gibbon and Christianity. London 1916. 17.

C. N. Cochrane, "The Mind of Edward Gibbon," 18.
   University of Toronto Quarterly, XII (1942),

Edward Gibbon

1-17.
See companion article, ibid., XII (1943), 146-66.

19. F. Cordasco, "Gibbon and the Gentleman's Magazine," Notes & Queries, CXCIV (1949), 254.

20. Lewis P. Curtis, "Gibbon's Paradise Lost" in The Age of Johnson. Essays presented to Chauncey Brewster Tinker, New Haven 1949, pp. 73-90.

21. Christopher Dawson, "Edward Gibbon," Proceedings of the British Academy 1934 (1936).

22. W. H. Graham, "Gibbon's Decline and Fall," Contemporary Review, September, 1946, pp. 106-10.

23. Frederick C. Grant, "Edward Gibbon's five causes," Religion in Life, XIII (1943), 1825.

24. R. T. Gunther, "Some unedited accounts of Gibbon," Notes & Queries, 25 August 1923; 1, 8 September 1923.

25. W. H. J. _____, "Gibbon and Johnson," Notes & Queries, CLXXIII (1937), 97.

26. E. Harrison, "Gibbon's Syntax," [London] Times Literary Supplement, February 22, 1941, p. 91.

27. Vernon P. Helming, "Edward Gibbon and Georges Deyverdun, collaborators in the Memoires Littéraires de la Grande Bretagne," Publications of the Modern Language Association of America, XLVII (1932), 1028-49.

28. Marjorie C. Hill, "A note on the Sheffield editions of Gibbon's Autobiography," Review of English Studies, XIV (1938), 440-46.

Edward Hutton, "The conversion of Edward   29.
    Gibbon," Nineteenth Century, CXI
    (1932), 362-75.

Geoffrey Keynes, "The Library of Edward   30.
    Gibbon," Library, XIX (1938), 155.
    Summary of a paper reprinted in No. 3.

Roger Lloyd, "Gibbon and the Christians,"   31.
    London Quarterly and Holborn Review,
    January 1937, pp. 41-50.

D. M. Low, Edward Gibbon, 1737-1794. London   32.
    1937.
    Rev. [London] Times Literary Supplement,
    20 March, 1937, p. 211.

_____, "Scribble, scribble, scribble!", 33.
    [London] Times Literary Supplement,
    22 January 1944, p. 43.
    A Gibbon anecdote.

I. W. J. Machin, "Gibbon's debt to contemporary   34.
    scholarship," Review of English Studies,
    XV (1939), 84-88.

Shelby T. McCloy, Gibbon's antagonism to   35.
    Christianity. University of North Carolina
    Press 1933.
    Rev. P. Smith, Americal Historical Review,
    XXXIX (1933), 167-68.

J. C. Morrison, Gibbon. English Men of Letters. 36.
    London 1878.

R. B. Mowat, Gibbon. London 1936.   37.
    Rev. P. Yvon, Revue Anglo-Américaine,
    XIII (1936), 437.

J. W. Oliver, "William Robertson and Edward   38.
    Gibbon," Scottish Historical Review,
    XXVI (1947), 86.

Charles D. O'Malley, "Some material on the death   39.
    of Edward Gibbon," Bulletin of the History
    of Medicine, XIII (1943), 200-09.

Edward Gibbon

40. L. F. Powell, "Friedrich von Matthison on Gibbon" in German Studies Presented to Professor H. G. Fiedler, Oxford 1938, pp. 345-51.

41. W. F. Rae, "Gibbon's Library," Athenaeum, June 1897.

42. J. M. Robertson, Gibbon. London 1925.

43. George Sampson, "Gibbon's proposal," [London] Times Literary Supplement, 9 June 1945, p. 271.

44. J. J. Saunders, "Gibbon and The Decline and Fall," History, XXIII (1939), 346-55.

45. James Smith, Junius Unveiled. London 1909. Argues Gibbon's authorship of the letters of Junius. For history of attribution of the letters of Junius to Gibbon see F. Cordasco, A Junius Bibliography, N.Y., 1949.

46. Joseph W. Swain, "Edward Gibbon and The Decline and Fall," South Atlantic Quarterly, XXXIX (1940), 77-93.

47. John Thomas, "Edward Gibbon and his circle portrayed by Wedgwood Medallions and busts," Apollo, XXVII (1938), 248-53.

48. A. Hamilton Thompson, Gibbon. London 1946.

49. James W. Thompson, "The library of Gibbon the historian," Library Quarterly, VII (1937), 343-53.

50. _____, "Edward Gibbon, 1737-1794," Pacific Historical Review, VII (1938), 93-119.

51. David Thomson, "Edward Gibbon: the master builder," Contemporary Review, CLI (1937), 583-91.

A. van de Put, "Gibboniana," [London] 52.
    Times Literary Supplement, 15 June 1933,
    p. 412.

J. H. Vince, "A passage in Gibbon," [London] 53.
    Times Literary Supplment, 1 February
    1941, p. 55.

G. M. Young, Gibbon. London 1932. 54.

"A Portrait of Gibbon," Oxford Magazine, 55.
    LVI (1938), 500-01.

"Portrait of an artist: the young Gibbon," 56.
    Cornhill, 1944, pp. 91-96; 252-60.

"Proceedings of the Gibbon Commemoration, 57.
    1794-1894," Royal Historical Society (1895).

"Remnant of Gibbon's Library," [London] 58.
    Times Literary Supplement, 27 December
    1934, p. 924.

"The Historian and 'the Gibbon'," [London] 59.
    Times Literary Supplement, 24 April
    1937, pp. 297-98.

XI.

Edward Young
A Handlist of Critical Notices & Studies

Copyright 1950 by Francesco Cordasco

Introductory Note

The main critical and biographical studies of Edward Young are gathered together in the present handlist. A list of the works is conveniently available in the <u>Cambridge Bibliography of English Literature</u> (1941), and the state of the bibliographical knowledge of the <u>Night Thoughts</u> is amply illustrated in the important articles of Professor Pettit listed <u>infra</u>. Like the other handlists, the present intends the collection of <u>important</u> criticism and if a study or book has been overlooked whose importance I have not realized I ask the student's indulgence. At best the compilation remains <u>un modesto saggio bibliographico</u> which will offer aid to the serious student of 18th Century cultural history. It is with this aim that the series was projected, and in the realisation of this aim that it is hoped its twenty numbers may be achieved.

F. C.

Part I.
General Bibliography

For general bibliography see The Cambridge Bibliography of English Literature, II, 290-292; Lowndes's Bibliographer's Manual (rev. Bohn, 1858-64); and particularly the work of Professor Henry Pettit listed infra.

Part II.
General Criticism and Biography

1. Nelson F. Adkins, "Emerson's 'Days' and Edward Young," Modern Language Notes, LXIII (1948), 269-71.

2. Margery Bailey, "Edward Young," in The Age of Johnson. Essays presented to Chauncey Brewster Tinker, New Haven, 1949, pp. 197-207.

3. F. Baldensperger, "Young et ses Nuits en France" in Etudes d'histoire littéraire, Paris 1907.

4. J. Barnstorff, Youngs Nachtgedanken und ihr Einfluss auf die deutsche Litteratur. Bamberg 1895.

5. Isabel St. John Bliss, "Young's Night Thoughts in relation to contemporary Christian apologetics," Publications of the Modern Language Association of America, XLIX (1934), 37-70.

6. F. S. Boas, "A ms. copy of Edward Young's Busiris, [London] Times Literary Supplement, 22 May 1930, p. 434.

7. Marjorie Bowen, "Edward Young," Transactions of the Royal Society of Literature, VIII (1928).

R. W. C[hapman], "Young's Night Thoughts," 8.
Review of English Studies, IV (1928), 330.
Dates of publication of Nights, IV-VI, VIII.

Hubert Clages, Der blankvers in Thomson's 9.
Seasons and Young's Night Thoughts.
Halle 1892.

H. H. Clark, "A study of melancholy in Edward 10.
Young," Modern Language Notes, XXXIX
(1924).

————, "The Romanticism of Edward Young". 11.
Reprinted from the Transactions of the
Wisconsin Academy of Sciences and Letters,
XXIV (1929).
Rev. Philological Quarterly, IX (1930),
203-205.

Charlotte E. Crawford, "Edward Young and the 12.
Wycombe election," Modern Language
Notes, LX (1945), 459-61.
Young's relations with George Bubb Dodington.

————, "What was Pope's debt to Edward 13.
Young?", ELH: A Journal of English
Literary History, XIII (1946), 157-67.

T. C. Duncan Eaves, "Joseph Highmore's por- 14.
trait of the Reverend Edward Young,"
Studies in Philology, XLIII (1946), 668-74.

T. W. Hanson, "Richard Edwards, publisher," 15.
[London] Times Literary Supplement,
8 August 1942, p. 396.
The publisher of the edition of Night Thoughts
illustrated by Blake.

Bruno Heeg, Edward Youngs gedicht Night 16.
Thoughts. Leipzig 1901.

W. R. Hughes, "Dr. Young and his curates," 17.
Blackwood's Magazine, CCXXVI (1932),
623-31.

C. H. Ibershoff, "Bodmer and Young," Journal 18.
of English and Germanic Philology,

XXIV (1925), pp. 211-18.

19. J. L. Kind, Edward Young in Germany. New York 1906.

20. K. Laux, Das Pseudoklassizistische und Romantische in Edward Youngs "Night Thoughts." Munich 1938.

21. A. D. McKillop, "Richardson, Young and the Conjectures," Modern Philology, XXII (1925).

22. H. Mutschmann, "Zur psychologie des verfassers der Nachtgedanken," Anglia Beiblatt, XXXIII (1922), 12-23.

23. _____, "Der schlüssel zu Youngs 'Nachtgedanken'" in Englische Kultur in sprachwissenschaftlicher Deutung. Max Deutschbein zum 60. Geburtstage. Leipzig 1936. (pp. 101-108).

24. _____, The origin and meaning of Young's Night Thoughts. (Acta et Commentationes Universitatis Tartuensis, B. XLIII. 5) Tartu 1939.
Notice in [London] Times Literary Supplement 12 August 1939, p. 482.

25. E. A. Peers, "The Influence of Young and Gray in Spain," Modern Language Review, XXI (1926), pp. 404-18.

26. Henry Pettit, "Young's Night Thoughts," [London] Times Literary Supplement, 14 October 1939, p. 593.

27. _____, "The Dating of Young's Night Thoughts," Modern Language Notes, LV (1940), 194-95.

28. _____, "The Text of Edward Young's letters to Samuel Richardson," Modern Language Notes, LVII (1942), 668-70.

29. _____, "Preface to a bibliography of Young's Night Thoughts," in Elizabethan Studies and other Essays in honor of George F. Reynolds (University of Colorado Studies in the Humanities, II, No. 4, 1945), pp. 215-22.

30. _____, "Young's Night Thoughts Reexamined," Library, 5th series, III, 299-301. Variants in early editions of the parts.

31. _____, "A Check list of Young's Night Thoughts in America," Papers of the Bibliographical Society of America, XLII (1948), 150-56. See additions, ibid., XLIV (1950). See also W. D. Templeman, ibid., XLIII (1949), 348-49.

32. H. C. Shelley, The Life and Letters of Edward Young. Boston 1914.

33. George Sherburn, "Edward Young and book advertising," Review of English Studies, IV (1928), 414-17.

34. Martin W. Steinke, Edward Young's Conjectures on Original Composition in England and Germany. New York 1917.

35. Peter Stubbs, "Edward Young and Locke's theory of perception," Notes and Queries, CLXXXVII (1944), 14-15.

36. H. T. Swedenberg, jr., "Letters of Edward Young to Mrs. Judith Reynolds," Huntington Library Quarterly, II (1938), 89-100.

37. H. E. von Teubern, Edward Youngs gedanken über die originalwerke in einem schreiben an Samuel Richardson. Bonn 1910.

38. W. Thomas, Le poète Edward Young. Paris 1901.

39. P. Van Tieghem, "La poésie de la nuit et des Tombeaux" in Le prêromantisme, ser. 2, Paris 1930.

XII.

Edmund Burke
A Handlist of Critical Notices & Studies

Copyright 1950 by Francesco Cordasco

Contents

I. General Bibliography 197

II. General Criticism and Biography 197

III. Miscellaneous 205

Note

This handlist gathers the main critical and biographical studies of Edmund Burke. I have provided a brief note on the general bibliography and in a miscellaneous division I have listed some items whose nature is incidental to the study of the statesman. The arrangement of the items is alphabetical by authors, and for some items reviews have been cited.

F. C.

I. General Bibliography

The Complete Works are edited by F. H. Willis and F. W. Rafferty (6v., 1906-08); the Correspondence is edited by E. Fitzwilliam and R. Bourke (4v., 1844). For general bibliography see Cambridge Bibliography of English Literature, II, 632-636; Lowndes's Bibliographer's Manual (rev. H. G. Bohn); and The R. B. Adam Library relating to Dr. Samuel Johnson & his era (3v., 1929-30). A full list of the works is in Prior, listed infra.

II. General Criticism and Biography

1. A. A. B[aumann], Burke, the founder of conservatism, London 1929.

2. Ernest Barker, Burke and Bristol: a study of the relations between Burke and his constituency during the years 1774-1780. Bristol 1931.

3. _____, "Edmund Burke et la révolution française," Revue Philosophique, CXXVIII (1939), 129-60.

4. Robert Bisset, Life of Edmund Burke. 2v. London 1800.

5. F. Braune, Edmund Burke in Deutschland. Heidelberg 1917.

6. Donald C. Bryant, "Edmund Burke on oratory," Quarterly Journal of Speech, XIX (1933), 1-18.

7. _____, "Edmund Burke's opinions of some orators of his day," Quarterly Journal of Speech, XX (1934), 241-54.

8. _____, "Burke's relations with writers and artists," Abstracts of theses, Cornell University, 1937 (1938), pp. 63-66.

_____, Edmund Burke and his literary friends. (Washington University Studies, Language and Literature, No. 9) St. Louis 1939. 9.

_____, "The contemporary reception of Edmund Burke's speaking," Studies in Honor of Frederick W. Shipley (Washington University Studies, New Series: Language and Literature, No. 14 [St. Louis 1942]), pp. 245-64. 10.

_____, "Edmund Burke's conversation," Studies in Speech and Drama in honor of Alexander M. Drummond (Cornell University Press, 1944), pp. 353-68. 11.

_____, "Edmund Burke and James Barry," Elizabethan Studies and other Essays in honor of George F. Reynolds (University of Colorado Studies...in the Humanities, II, No. 4, 1945), pp. 244-53. 12.

R. G. Beuhler, "Burke and Rousseau," Harvard University Summaries of Theses, 1934, pp. 313-14. 13.

Peter Burke, The public and domestic life of the Right Honourable Edmund Burke. London 1853. 14.

H. M. Butler, The Character of Edmund Burke, London 1854. 15.

I. Capadose, Edmund Burke. Amsterdam 1857. 16.

P. L. Carver, "Burke and the totalitarian system," University of Toronto Quarterly, XII (1942), 32-47. 17.

G. Chadwick, "Edmund Burke," Peplographia Dubliniensis (1902). 18.

F. H. Clack, The Character of Edmund Burke. London 1845. 19.

James L. Clifford, "Fanny Burney meets Edmund Burke," [London] Times Literary Supplement, 23 July, 1938, p. 493. 20.

Edmund Burke

21. Alfred Cobban, "Edmund Burke and the origins of the theory of nationality," Cambridge Historical Journal, II (1926), 36-47.

22. _____, Edmund Burke and the revolt against the 18th century: a study of the political and social thinking of Burke, Wordsworth, Coleridge, and Southey. London 1929. Rev. [London] Times Literary Supplement, 12 December 1929, p. 1052.

23. Padraic Colum, "Burke and the present order," Saturday Review of Literature, X (1933), pp. 141-42.

24. Carl B. Cone, "Pamphlet replies to Burke's Reflections," Southwestern Social and Science Quarterly, XXVI (1945), 22-34.

25. _____, "Edmund Burke, the farmer," Agricultural History, XIX (1945), 65-69.

26. Thomas W. Copeland, "Burke's Vindication of Natural Society," Library, XVIII (1938), 461-62.

27. _____, "Burke and Dodsley's Annual Register," Publications of the Modern Language Association of America, LIV (1939), 223-45.

28. _____, "Edmund Burke and the book reviews in Dodsley's Annual Register," Publications of the Modern Language Association of America, LVII (1942), 446-68.

29. _____, Our Eminent friend, Edmund Burke: Six Essays. New Haven 1949.

30. G. Croly, Memoirs of the political life of Edmund Burke, 2v. London 1840.

31. Edward Dowden, The French Revolution and English literature. New York 1897.

32. Helen L. Drew, "The Date of Burke's Sublime and Beautiful," Modern Language Notes, L (1935), 510-21.

33. Charles Eden, "Edmund Burke, 1797-1947," Contemporary Review, CLXXII (1947), 99-102.

34. Mario Einaudi, "The British background of Burke's political philosophy," Political Science Quarterly, XLIX (1934), 576-98.

35. Eugenis Garin, Introduzione alla dottrina politica di Burke. (Quaderni di Critica, XII) Firenze [1938].

36. P. Guedalla, "Mr. Burke and the grand manner," Nation, 30 January; 6 February 1926.

37. Denis Gwynn, "Dr. Hussey and Edmund Burke," Studies: an Irish Quarterly Review, XVII (1928), 529-46.

38. Victor M. Hamm, "Burke and metaphysics," New Scholasticism, XVIII (1944), 3-18.

39. W. G. Howard, "Burke among the forerunners of Lessing," Publications of the Modern Language Association of America, XXII (1907), 608-32.

40. Robert M. Hutchins, "The Theory of oligarchy, Edmund Burke," Thomist, V (1943), 61-78.

41. _____, "The Theory of the state, Edmund Burke," Review of Politics, V (1943), 139-55.

42. W. H. J____, "Burke's classical jest," Notes & Queries, CLXXXIII (1942), 134.

43. Harro de W. Jensen, "Das konservative Weet-und Staatsbild Edmund Burkes," Anglia, LVIII (1934), 155-224.
Notice in Philological Quarterly, XIV (1935), 159-60.

44. Heinz Krieger, "Die Bedeutung des Organischen im englischen Volks-und Stattsbegriff (Burke, Freeman, Seeley, Froude)," Die Neueren Sprachen, XLVI (1938), 1-16.

Edmund Burke 201

45. R. Lennox, Edmund Burke und sein politisches Arbeitfeld in den Jahren 1760-1790. Berlin 1923.

46. John A. Lester, Jr., "An Analysis of the conservative thought of Edmund Burke," Harvard University... Summaries of Theses... 1943-45 (1947), pp. 460-62.

47. Klaus Luhn, Angelsächische Berichterstattung. Die Berichterstattung über die Ereignisse der Französischen Revolution bei Burke, Paine, Mackintosh, und Young. Frankfort 1941.
Rev. H. Marcus, Die Neueren Sprachen, XLIX (1941), 127-28.

48. John MacCunn, The Political philosophy of Burke. New York 1913.

49. T. MacKnight, History of the life and times of Edmund Burke. 3v. London 1858-60.

50. Sir Philip Magnus, Edmund Burke: A Life. London 1939.
Rev. F. J. C. Hearnshaw, History, XXIV, 271-72.

51. _____, "Finances of Edmund Burke; unpublished documents," [London] Times Literary Supplement, 6 May 1939, p. 272.

52. _____, "Edmund Burke," Oriel Review [I 1943], 117-24.

53. Thomas D. Mahoney, "Edmund Burke and Ireland," George Washington University Summaries of Doctoral Dissertations, 1944-46 (1947), pp. 20-26.

54. Somerset Maugham, "On Style (after reading Burke)" Decision, I (1941), 28-37.

55. F. Meusel, Edmund Burke und die französische Revolution. Berlin 1913.

M. F. K. Millar, "Burke and the moral basis of political liberty," Thought, XVI (1941), 79-101.   56.

J. Morley, Edmund Burke, an historical Study. London 1867.   57.

_____, Edmund Burke (English Men of Letters). London 1879.   58.

Robert H. Murray, Edmund Burke, a biography. Oxford 1931.
Rev. Contemporary Review, CXL (1931), 661-63.   59.

Bertram Newman, Edmund Burke. London 1927.
Rev J. Vallette, Les Langues Modernes, XXV (1927), 558-61.   60.

William O'Brien, Edmund Burke as an Irishman. Dublin 1924. 2nd ed. 1926.   61.

Robert T. Oliver, Four who spoke out: Burke, Fox, Sheridan, Pitt. Syracuse: Syracuse University Press 1946.
Rev. W. F. Woodring, American Historical Review, LIII (1946), 157.   62.

F. von Oppenheimer, Edmund Burke und die französische Revolution. Berlin 1928.   63.

C. W. Opzoomer, Conservatismus und reform: eine Abhandlung über Edmund Burke Politik. Utrecht 1852.   64.

Annie M. Osborn, Rousseau and Burke: a study of the idea of liberty in 18th century political thought. New York 1940.
Rev. H. V. S. Ogden, American Historical Review, XLVI (1940), 899-900.   65.

E. A. Pankhurst, Edmund Burke: a study of his life and character. London 1886.   66.

T. D. Pillans, Edmund Burke, apostle of justice and liberty. London 1905.   67.

Edmund Burke

68. Sir James Prior, Memoir of the life and character of the Right Honourable Edmund Burke. London 1824. 5th ed. 1854. Contains a valuable list of Burke's works. Reprinted in Bohn's Standard Library.

69. Brother J. Robert, "Toleration for Catholics: the mind of Burke," Thought, XIV (1939), 633-43.

70. J. B. Robertson, Lectures on the life, writings and times of Edmund Burke. Dublin [1869].

71. J. Roche, An Enquiry concerning the author of the letters of Junius; in which it is proved that they were written by the late Rt. Hon. Edmund Burke. London 1813. Burke's claim was also argued by Patrick Kelly (1826). For history of attribution of letters to Burke, see F. Cordasco, A Junius Bibliography, N. Y., 1949.

72. A. P. Samuels, Early life, correspondence and writings of Edmund Burke. Cambridge 1923.

73. H. V. F. Somerset, "Burke's eloquence and Hansard's reports," English Review, LII (1931), 342-50.

74. _____, "Burke and the Cavendishes," English Historical Review, XLVII (1932), 280-86.

75. _____, "Edmund Burke, England and the Papacy," Dublin Review, CII (1938), 138-48. Contains an unpublished letter of Burke.

76. _____, "Edmund Burke outside politics," Dublin Review, CCIV (1939), 140-46.

77. _____, "Burke's workmanship," English, II (1939), 234-40.

78. _____, "Edmund Burke as a letter writer," Nineteenth Century, CXL (1946), 94-97.

79. N. Spinelli, The Political life of Edmund Burke. London 1908.

80. C. Stebbins, "Edmund Burke as agent of New York," Proceedings of the American Antiquarian Society, IX (1893).

81. L. S. Sutherland, "Edmund Burke and the first Rockingham ministry," English Historical Review, XLVII (1932), 46-72.

82. Andrew Tomlinson, "An unpublished letter of Burke's," [London] Times Literary Supplement, 10 January 1929, p. 28. Cf. Ibid., 17 January 1929, p. 44.

83. G. F. Weare, Edmund Burke's connection with Bristol, 1774-80 Bristol 1894.

84. Dixon Wecter, "Burke's birthday," Notes & Queries, CLXXII (1937), 441.

85. _____, "Adam Smith and Burke," Notes & Queries, CLXXIV (1938), 310-11.

86. _____, "Goldsmith and the Burkes," [London] Times Literary Supplement, 12 February 1938, p. 108.

87. _____, "Four letters from George Crabbe to Edmund Burke," Review of English Studies, XIV (1938), 298-309.

88. _____, "Four unpublished letters from Boswell to Burke," Modern Philology, XXXVI (1938), 47-58.

89. _____, "Two notes on the biography of Edmund Burke," Notes & Queries, CLXXV (1938), 417-18.

90. _____, "the missing years in Edmund Burke's biography," Publications of the Modern Language Association of America, LIII (1938), 1102-25.

Edmund Burke

91. _____, "Burke's prospective duel," Notes & Queries, CLXXIV (1938), 186-87; 296-97.

92. _____, Edmund Burke and his kinsmen. A study of the statesman's financial integrity and private relationships. (University of Colorado Studies, Series B...vol. I, No. 1) Boulder 1939.
Rev. [London] Times Literary Supplement, 8 July 1939, 412.

93. _____, "David Garrick and the Burkes," Philological Quarterly, XVIII (1939), 367-80.

94. _____, "Sir Joshua Reynolds and the Burkes," Philological Quarterly, XVIII (1939), 301-05.

95. _____, "Horace Walpole and Edmund Burke," Modern Language Notes, LIV (1939), 124-26.

96. _____, "Burke's error regarding sugar crystals," Modern Language Notes, LV (1940), 47-50.

97. _____, "Burke, Franklin and Samuel Petrie," Huntington Library Quarterly, III (1940), 315-38.

98. _____, "Burke's theory of words, images and emotions," Publications of the Modern Language Association of America, LV (1940), 167-81.

99. G. M. Young, "An Essay by Burke," [London] Times Literary Supplement, 3 August 1940, p. 375.
Cf. Ibid., 10 August 1940, p. 387.

III. Miscellaneous

100. A Catalogue of the collection of antique statues and other marbles and Italian pictures the property of the Rt. Hon. Edmund Burke. London 1812.

"The Bicentenary of Burke," [London] Times Literary Supplement, 10 January 1929, pp. 17-18.   101.

"Edmund Burke's empire," [London] Times Literary Supplement, 20 December, 1947, p. 661.   102.

Ernest Barker, Essays on government. New York 1945.   103.

G. G. Butler, The Tory tradition. London 1914.   104.

R. J. S. Hoffman and Paul Levack (eds.), Burke's politics. Selected writings and speeches of Edmund Burke on reform, revolution and war. New York 1949.   105.

Wyndham Papers. With an introduction by the Earl of Rosebery. 2v. London 1913. See also Wyndham's Diary (1784-1810), ed. H. Baring, 1866.   106.

Appendix

Bibliography of Tobias George Smollett
by John P. Anderson (British Museum)

Contents

I.	Works	211
II.	Poetical Works	212
III.	Selections	213
IV.	Single Works	213
V.	Translations	220
VI.	Miscellaneous	222
VII.	Appendix--	
	Biography, Criticism, etc	222
	Magazine Articles	228
VIII.	Chronological List of Works	229

I. Works

1. The Miscellaneous Works of Tobias Smollett.
    With a short account of the author [and frontispieces by Rowlandson]. 6 vols. Edinburgh, 1790, 8vo.
    Reprinted with the same plates, Edinburgh, 1809, in 5 vols., 8vo.

2. The Miscellaneous Works of T. S., with Memoirs of his Life and Writings, by R. Anderson. 6 vols. London, 1796, 8vo.

3. _____Another edition. 6 vols. 1806, 8vo.

4. _____Another edition. 6 vols. Edinburgh, 1811, 8vo.

5. _____Fifth edition, with portrait of Smollett. 6 vols. Edinburgh, 1817, 8vo.

6. The Miscellaneous Works of T. S. Sixth edition. 6 vols. Edinburgh, 1820, 8vo.

7. _____Another edition. 12 vols. London, 1824, 12mo.

8. The Works of T. S., with memoirs of his life, to which is prefixed a view of the commencement and progress of romance, by J. Moore. 8 vols. London, 1797, 8vo.

9. _____Another edition, edited by J. P. Browne. 8 vols. London, 1872, 8vo.

10. The Miscellaneous Works of T. S., complete in one volume, with memoir of the author, by Thomas Roscoe. London, 1841, 8vo.

11. The Miscellaneous Works of T. S. Another edition, illustrated by George Cruikshank. London, 1845, 8vo.

The Works of T. S., carefully selected and   12.
    edited from the best authorities, with
    numerous original historical notes and
    a life of the author, by David Herbert.
    Edinburgh, 1870 [1869], 8vo.

II. Poetical Works

The Poetical Work of Tobias Smollett, to   13.
    which is prefixed the life of the author
    (Anderson's Poets of Great Britain, vol. x.).
    Edinburgh, 1794, 8vo.

The Poetical Works of T. S., collated with the   14.
    best editions, by Thomas Park (Works
    of the British Poets, vol. xli.). London,
    1808, 16mo.

The Poems of T. S., with a life by Mr. Chalmers 15.
    (Works of the English Poets, vol. xv.).
    London, 1810, 8vo.

Select Poems of T. S., with a life of the Author 16.
    (Works of the British Poets, vol. xxxiii).
    Boston [U. S.], 1822, 12mo.

The Poems of T. S. The life by S. W. Singer   17.
    (British Poets, vol. lxvi). Chiswick,
    1822, 12mo.

The Poetical Works of Oliver Goldsmith, Tobias   18.
    Smollett, etc. Illustrated by John Gilbert.
    (Routledge's British Poets.) London, 1853,
    8vo.

The Poetical Works of Johnson, Parnell, Gray,   19.
    and Smollett. With memoirs, critical
    dissertations, and explanatory notes, by
    the Rev. George Gilfillan. Edinburgh,
    1855, 8vo.

The Poetical Works of Johnson, Parnell, Gray,   20.
    and Smollett. Another edition. The text
    edited by C. C. Clarke. London [1878], 8vo.

The Poetical Works of Oliver Goldsmith, Tobias   21.
    Smollett, Samuel Johnson, and William

Shenstone, with biographical notices and notes. London [1881], 8vo.

III. Selections

The Beauties of the Magazines, consisting of essays, moral tales, etc., by Colman, Goldsmith, Murphy, Smollett, etc. 2 vols. London, 1772, 12mo.   22.

_____ Another edition. 2 vols. London, 1775, 8vo.   23.

Plays and Poems written by T. S., with memoirs of the life and writings of the author. London, 1777, 8vo.   24.

_____ Another edition. 1784, 8vo.   25.

The Novels of Tobias Smollett, to which is prefixed a memoir of the life of the author, by Sir Walter Scott. (Novelists' Library, vols. ii., iii.) 2 vols. London, 1821, 8vo.   26.

Illustrations of Smollett, Fielding, and Goldsmith, in a series of forty-one plates, designed and engraved by George Cruikshank. Accompanied by descriptive extracts. London, 1832, 8vo.   27.

The Beauties of Smollett, consisting of selections from his prose and poetry, by A. Howard. London [1834], 12mo.   28.

IV. Single Works

Advice; a Satire [in verse, by T. S.]. London, 1746, fol.   29.

Reproof; a Satire [in verse]. The Sequel to Advice. London, 1747, fol.   30.

Advice and Reproof; two Satires first published in the year 1746 and 1747. London, 1748, 4to.   31.

———————— Another edition (British Satirist). 32.
Glasgow, 1826, 12mo.

The Adventures of Roderick Random. 2 vols. 33.
London, 1748, 12mo.

———————— Third edition. 2 vols. London, 34.
1750, 12mo.

———————— Seventh edition. 2 vols. London, 35.
1766, 12mo.

———————— Eighth edition. 2 vols. London, 36.
1770, 12mo.

———————— Tenth edition. 2 vols. London, 37.
1778, 8vo.

———————— Another edition. 2 vols. London, 38.
1780, 12mo.

———————— Twelfth edition. 2 vols. London, 39.
1784, 8vo.

———————— Another edition, abridged by R. Lewis. 40.
Dublin, 1791, 12mo.

———————— Another edition, with the life of the 41.
author. 2 vols. London [1793], 12mo.
Vols. viii. and ix. of a series entitled
"Cooke's edition of Select British Novels."

———————— Another edition (Walker's Classics). 42.
London, 1815, 24mo.

———————— Another edition, with illustrations 43.
by George Cruikshank. (Roscoe's
Novelist's Library, vol. ii.) London,
1831, 12mo.

———————— Another edition. (Tauchnitz Collec- 44.
tion of British Authors, vol. lxxxviii.)
Leipzig, 1845, 16mo.

———————— Another edition. With a memoir of 45.
the author [by G. H. T. --i. e., G. H. Town-
send]. London, 1857, 8vo.

Smollett Bibliography 215

46. _____ Another edition, illustrated by George Cruikshank. London, 1836, 12 mo.

47. The Adventures of Roderick Random. Another edition. London [1867], 8vo.
One of a series, entitled "Routledge's Railway Library."

48. The Regicide: or James the First of Scotland. A Tragedy, by the author of Roderick Random. London, 1749, 8vo.

49. The Adventures of Peregrine Pickle. In which are included, Memoirs of a Lady of Quality. 4 vols. London, 1751, 12 mo.

50. _____ Second edition. London, 1751, 12mo.

51. _____ Third edition. 4 vols. London, 1765, 12mo.

52. _____ Fourth edition. 4 vols. London, 1769, 12mo.

53. _____ Fifth edition. 4 vols. London, 1773, 12mo.

54. _____ Another edition. 4 vols. London, 1781, 8vo.
The pagination is continuous throughout the 4 vols.

55. _____ Seventh edition. 4 vols. London, 1784, 12mo.

56. _____ Cooke's edition. 4 vols. London [1794], 12mo.
One of a series entitled "Cooke's edition of Select British Novels."

57. _____ Another edition. With plates by Rowlandson. 4 vols. Edinburgh, 1805, 8vo.

58. _____ Another edition. 2 vols. London, 1815, 12mo.
Each volume has an engraved title-page and frontispiece. This forms part of "Walker's British Classics."

_____ Another edition, with illustrations 59.
by George Cruikshank. (Roscoe's
Novelist's Library, vols. iii., iv.) 2 vols.
London, 1831, 12mo.

_____ Another edition. With illustrations 60.
by Phiz. London, 1857, 8vo.

The Adventures of Peregrine Pickle. Another 61.
edition. 2 vols. London, 1882, 8vo.
One of "Routledge's Sixpenny Novels."

_____ Another edition. London, 1882, 8vo. 62.

Essay on the external use of Water, with 63.
particular remarks on the mineral waters
of Bath. London, 1752, 4to.

A Faithful Narrative of the base and inhuman 64.
arts that were lately practised upon the
brain of Habbakkuk Hilding [i.e., Henry
Fielding], Justice, Dealer, and Chapman.
By Drawcansir Alexander [i.e. Tobias
Smollett]. London, 1752, 8vo.

The Adventures of Ferdinand, Count Fathom. 65.
[By T.S.] 2 vols. London, 1753, 12mo.

_____ Second edition. 2 vols. London, 66.
1771, 12mo.

_____ Another edition. 2vols. London, 67.
1780, 12mo.

_____ Another edition. 2vols. London, 68.
1782, 8vo.
The pagination is continuous throughout
the 2 vols.

_____ Another edition. London [1795], 12mo. 69.
One of a series, entitled "Cooke's edition
of Select British Novels."

A Compendium of Authentic and Entertaining 70.
Voyages digested in a Chronological Series,
etc. [Edited by T. Smollett.] 7 vols.
London, 1756, 12mo.

Smollett Bibliography

71. _____ Second edition. 7 vols. London, 1766, 12mo.

72. The Reprisal: or, the Tars of Old England. A Comedy [by T. S.] of two acts, as performed at the Theatre Royal in Drury Lane. London, 1757, 8vo.

73. A Compleat History of England, deduced from the descent of Julius Caesar to the Treaty of Aix-la-Chapelle, 1748, containing the transactions of one thousand eight hundred and three years. 4 vols. London, 1757-58, 4to.

74. _____ Second edition. 11 vols. London, 1758-60, 8vo.

75. _____ Continuation of the Complete History of England. 5 vols. London, 1763-65, 8vo.

76. _____ The History of England from the Revolution to the death of George the Second. (Designed as a continuation of Mr. Hume's History.) A new edition. 5 vols. London, 1789, 8vo. Numerous subsequent editions.

77. The Adventures of Sir Launcelot Greaves, by the author of Roderick Random. 2 vols. London, 1762, 12mo. Originally appeared in the British Magazine for 1760-61, when the author was in prison for a libel in the Critical Review on Admiral Knowles.

78. _____ Another edition. 2 vols. London, 1774, 12mo.

79. _____ Another edition. 2 vols. London, 1780, 12mo.

80. _____ Another edition. 2 vols. London, 1782, 8vo. The pagination is continuous throughout the 2 vols.

————— Another edition. 2 vols. London, 1783, 12mo.   81.

————— Another edition. 2 vols. London, 1793, 12mo.   82.

————— Another edition. London, 1810, 24 mo. There is also an engraved title-page dated 1809.   83.

————— Another edition, with illustrations by George Cruikshank. (Roscoe's Novelist's Library, vol. x.) London, 1832, 12mo.   84.

The Present State of all Nations. Containing a geographical, natural, commerical, and political history of all the countries in the known world. 8 vols. London, 1764, 8vo.   85.

————— Another edition. 8 vols. London, 1768-9, 8vo.   86.

Travels through France and Italy, etc. 2 vols. London, 1766, 8vo. The British Museum possesses a copy with MS. notes by the author.   87.

————— Second edition. 2 vols. Dublin, 1772, 12mo.   88.

————— Another edition. 2 vols. London, 1778, 12mo.   89.

The History and Adventures of an Atom. By Nathaniel Peacock [i.e., Tobias Smollett]. 2 vols. London, 1749 [1769], 12mo.   90.

————— Another edition. 2 vols. London, 1769, 12mo.   91.

————— Tenth edition. 2 vols. London, 1778, 12mo.   92.

————— Another edition. 2 vols. Edinburgh, 1784, 12mo.   93.

Smollett Bibliography

_____ Another edition. 2 vols. London, 1786, 8vo. The pagination is continuous throughout the 2 vols.	94.
The Expedition of Humphry Clinker, by the author of Roderick Random. 3 vols. London, 1671 [1771], 12mo.	95.
_____ Second edition. 3 vols. London, 1772, 12mo.	96.
_____ Another edition. 2 vols. Edinburgh, 1788, 12mo.	97.
_____ Fourth edition. 3 vols. London, 1792, 12mo.	98.
_____ Another edition. 2 vols. London [1794], 12mo. One of a series, entitled "Cooke's edition of Select British Novels."	99.
_____ Another edition. 2 vols. London, 1805, 8vo.	100.
The Expedition of Humphry Clinker. Another edition. London, 1808, 12mo. With a second and engraved title-page.	101.
_____ Another edition. (British Novelists, vols. xxx., xxxi.) 2 vols. London, 1810, 12mo.	102.
_____ Another edition. London, 1815, 24mo.	103.
_____ Another edition. With illustrations by George Cruikshank. (Roscoe's Novelist's Library, vol. 1.) London, 1831, 12mo.	104.
_____ Another edition. (Tauchnitz Collection, vol. xcii.) Leipzig, 1846, 16mo.	105.
_____ Another edition. With illustrations by Phiz [i.e., H. K. Browne]. London, 1857, 8vo.	106.

219

_____Another edition. London, 1882, 8vo. 107.

<u>Ode to Independence.</u> With notes and observa- 108.
    tions. Glasgow, 1773, 4to.

_____Another edition. London, 1774, 4to. 109.

_____Another edition. Glasgow [1800], 12mo. 110.

V. Translations

<u>The Adventures of Gil Blas of Santillane.</u> 111.
    A new translation [by T. S.] from the
    best French edition. 4 vols. London,
    1749, 12mo.

_____Another edition. 4 vols. London, 112.
    1750, 12mo.

_____Another edition. 4 vols. London, 113.
    1761, 12mo.

_____Fourth edition. London, 1773, 12mo. 114.
    Other editions:
    London, 1780, 24mo, in 8 vols.;
    London, 1781, 12mo, in 4 vols.;
    Dublin, 1785, 12mo, in 4 vols.;
    London, 1789, 12mo, in 4 vols.;
    London, 1792, in 4 vols.;
    London [1793], 12mo, in 4 vols.;
    London, 1797, 12mo, in 4 vols.;
    London, 1818, 12mo, in 2 vols.;
    London, 1819, 8vo, in 3 vols.;
    London, 1826, 12mo, in 4 vols.;
    London, 1836, 8vo, in 2 vols., illustrated
    by Gigoux;
    London, 1835, 8vo, edited by T. Roscoe,
    illustrated by G. Cruikshank;
    London, 1841, 8vo, illustraded;
    London, 1866, 8vo;
    London, 1881, 8vo, in 3 vols., preceded
    by a biographical and critical notice of
    Lesage, by George Saintsbury, with twelve
    original etchings by R. de Los Rios.

<u>The History and Adventures of the renowned</u> 115.

Don Quixote. Translated from the
Spanish of M. de Cervantes Saavedra.
To which is prefixed an account of the
author's life. By T. S. [Illustrated with
twenty-eight plates designed by Hayman.]
2 vols. London, 1755, 4to.

———— Second edition. 4 vols. London, 116.
1761, 8vo.

———— Fifth edition. 4 vols. London, 117.
1782, 12mo.

———— Sixth edition. 4 vols. London, 118.
1792, 12mo.

———— Sixth edition corrected. 4 vols. 119.
London, 1793, 12mo.

———— Another edition. 4 vols. Dublin, 120.
1796, 8vo.

———— Another edition. 5 vols. London 121.
[1799], 12mo.

———— Another edition, abridged [from 122.
Smollett's translation]. Halifax, 1839,
16mo.

The Works of M. de Voltaire. Translated 123.
from the French. With notes, historical
and critical. [With portraits and frontis-
pieces.] By Dr. Smollet and others.
38 vols. London, 1761-1774, 12mo.
All volumes, with the exception of the
first, bear the name of Dr. T. Francklin
in addition to that of Dr. Smollett on the
title-page.

———— A new edition. London, 1778, etc., 124.
12mo.

The Adventures of Telemachus, the son of 125.
Ulysses. Translated from the French
by T. S. 2 vols. London, 1776, 12mo.

VI. Miscellaneous

126.   ―――― Another edition. 2 vols. Dublin, 1793, 12mo.

127. The Modern Part of an Universal History, from the earliest account of Time. Compiled from original writers by the authors of the Ancient Part. 44 vols. London, 1759-66, 8vo.
Smollett assisted in the compilation of this work, and is supposed, among other articles, to have contributed the Histories of France, Italy, and Germany.

128. The Tears of Scotland. Written in the year 1746.
This Ode was first printed without the author's name in "A Collection of the most esteemed Pieces of Poetry that have appeared for several years: with variety of originals, by the late Moses Mendez." London, 1767, 12mo.

129. The Critical Review; or, Annals of Literature. By a Society of Gentlemen. [Edited by T. Smollett.] London, 1756, etc., 8vo.

130. The British Magazine, or Monthly Repository for Gentlemen and Ladies. [Edited by T. Smollett, assisted by Oliver Goldsmith.] 8 vols. London [1760-67], 8vo.

131. The Briton. [Edited by T. S.] London (1762-63), fol.

VII. Appendix

Biography, Criticism, etc.

132. Anderson, Robert, The Life of Tobias Smollett, with critical observations on his works. London, 1796, 8vo.

Smollett Bibliography

Anderson, Robert, <u>The Life of Tobias Smollett.</u> Second edition. Edinburgh, 1800, 8vo. — 133.

_____ Fourth edition. Edinburgh, 1803, 8vo. — 134.

_____ Fifth edition. Edinburgh, 1806, 8vo. — 135.

Anderson, William, <u>The Scotish Nation;</u> or, the surnames, families, literature, honours, and biographical history of the people of Scotland. 3 vols. Edinburgh, 1863, 8vo.
Tobias Smollett, with portrait, vol. iii., pp. 483-485. — 136.

British Plutarch, <u>The British Plutarch,</u> containing the Lives of the most eminent Statesmen, etc. Third edition. 8 vols. London, 1791, 8vo.
Life of Dr. Tobias Smollett, vol. viii., pp. 117-128. — 137.

Carlyle, Rev. Dr. Alexander, <u>Autobiography of the Rev. Dr. A. Carlyle.</u> Edinburgh, 1860, 8vo.
References to T. S. in chaps. iv., vii., and ix. — 138.

Cary, Henry Francis, <u>Lives of the English Poets from Johnson to Kirke White.</u> London, 1846, 8vo.
Tobias Smollett, pp. 119-146. — 139.

Cervantes Saaverda, M. de, <u>Remarks</u> on the proposals lately published [by T. S.] for a new translation of <u>Don Quixote</u>, etc. London, 1755, 8vo. — 140.

Chambers, Robert, <u>Favourite Authors.</u> Smollett: his life and a selection from his writings. London, 1867, 8vo. — 141.

_____ <u>A Biographical Dictionary of eminent Scotsmen</u>. New edition, revised by the Rev. T. Thomson. London, 1870, 8vo. — 142.

Tobias Smollett, vol. iii., pp. 380-385.

Chambers, Robert,   Traditions of Edinburgh.   143.
   New Edition.   London, 1869, 8vo.
   Smollett's visit to Edinburgh, p. 323.

Comber, Thomas,   A Vindication of the Great   144.
   Revolution in England in 1688... with a
   confutation of the character of King
   James the Second, as misrepresented
   by the author [Dr. S.] of the complete
   history of England.   London, 1758, 8vo.

Davis, William,   A Second Journey round the   145.
   Library of a Bibliomaniac, etc.   London,
   1825, 8vo.
   Key to Smollett's History and Adventures
   of an Atom, pp. 115-118.

Dibdin, Thomas,   Humphry Clinker: a farce,   146.
   in two acts, by T. D.   London, [1828],
   12mo.
   In vol. iv. of Cumberland's Minor Theatre.

Encyclopaedia Britannica,   Encyclopaedia   147.
   Britannica.   Ninth edition.   Edinburgh,
   1887, 4to.
   T. Smollett, by Professor Minto,
   vol. xxii., pp. 183-185.

Forster, John,   The Life and Times of Oliver   148.
   Goldsmith.   Second edition.   2 vols.
   London, 1854, 8vo.
   References to T. S.

Forsyth, William,   The Novels and Novelists   149.
   of the Eighteenth Century, etc.   London,
   1871, 8vo.
   Smollett, pp. 278-303.

Frail, Lady,   A Parallel between the Charac-   150.
   ters of Lady Frail and the Lady of
   Quality in Peregrine Pickle.   In which
   the facts alledged in both are stated and
   compared, the character of the heroine
   set in a true light; the several other
   characters examined, etc. London, 1751, 8vo.

Smollett Bibliography

151. Frail, Lady, <u>An apology</u> for the conduct of a Lady of Quality [i.e., Anne, Viscountess Vane] lately traduc'd under the name of Lady Frail; wherein her case is fairly stated. In a letter from a person of honour, etc. London, 1751, 8vo.

152. Grainger, J., <u>A letter to Tobias Smollett,</u> occasioned by his criticism upon a late translation of Tibullus. London, 1759, 8vo.

153. Grant, James, <u>Cassell's Old and New Edinburgh.</u> 3 vols. London, 1882, 4to. References to Smollett.

154. Hazlitt, William, <u>Lectures on the English Comic Writers.</u> London, 1819, 8vo. T. Smollett, pp. 229-233.

155. Henderson, Andrew, <u>A second letter to Dr. Samuel Johnson...with an impartial character of Doctor Smollett,</u> etc. London [1775], 8vo.

156. Hill, J., <u>The History of a Woman of Quality;</u> or, the Adventures of Lady Frail [i.e., Anne, Viscountess Vane]. By an impartial hand [J. Hill]. London, 1751, 12mo.

157. Hillard, George Stillman, <u>Six Months in Italy.</u> 2 vols. London, 1853, 8vo. Smollett, vol. ii., pp. 295-298.

158. Hutton, Laurence, <u>Literary Landmarks of London.</u> London [1885], 8vo. Tobias Smollett, pp. 280-282.

159. Irving, J., <u>Some account of the Family of Smollett of Bonhill;</u> with a series of letters hitherto unpublished, written by Dr. Tobias Smollett. Dumbarton, 1859, 4to.

160. Irving, J., <u>The Book of Dumbartonshire;</u> a history of the country, burghs, parishes, and lands, memoirs of families, and notices of industries carried on in the

Lennox District. 3 vols. Edinburgh,
1879, 4to.
Family of Smollett of Bonhill, vol. ii.,
pp. 175-208.

Jeaffreson, J. Cordy, Novels and Novelists 161.
from Elizabeth to Victoria. 2 vols.
London, 1858, 8vo.
T. Smollett, vol. i., pp. 148-179.

Masson, David, British Novelists and their 162.
styles; being a critical sketch of the
history of British prose fiction.
Cambridge, 1859, 8vo.
Smollett, pp. 104-107; Fielding and
Smollett, pp. 128-145.

Montagu, Lady M. W., The Letters and Works 163.
of Lady M. W. Montagu. 2 vols.
London, 1861, 8vo.
References to T. S.

Nichols, John, Literary Anecdotes of the 164.
Eighteenth Century, etc. 9 vols.
London, 1812-1815, 8vo.
Numerous references to T. S.

Nicoll, Henry J., Landmarks of English 165.
Literature. London, 1883, 8vo.
T. Smollett, pp. 222-228.

Notes and Queries, General Index to Notes 166.
and Queries. Five series. London,
1856-1880, 4to.
Numerous references to T. S.

Prophecies, Wonderful Prophecies; being a 167.
dissertation on the existence, nature,
and extent of the prophetic powers in
the human mind; and a remarkable
prophecy of Dr. Smollett, just before
his death, etc. London, 1795, 8vo.

Reed, Joseph, A Sop in the Pan for a 168.
physical critick; in a letter to Dr.
Sm*ll*t [i.e., Tobias Smollett] occasion'd

Smollett Bibliography

by a criticism on a late Mock-Tragedy, call'd Madrigal and Trulletta. By a Halter-maker [i.e., Joseph Reed]. London, 1759, 8vo.

169. Scott, Sir Walter, A Memoir of the life of Tobias Smollett. (Prefixed to the Novels of T. S. in the Novelist's Library, vols. ii. and iii.) London, 1821, 8vo.

170. Shebbeare, Dr. John, The Occasional Critic; or, the decrees of the Scotch tribunal in the Critical Review rejudged. [By Dr. J. Shebbeare.] [London, 1757], 8vo.

171. Taine, H. A., Histoire de la Littérature Anglaise. 4 tom. Paris, 1863-64, 8vo. Smollett, tom. iii., pp. 318-324.

172. History of English Literature. Translated by H. van Laun. New Edition. 4 vols. Edinburgh, 1873-74, 8vo. Smollett, vol. iii., pp. 300-306.

173. Thackeray, W. M., The English Humourists of the Eighteenth Century. Second edition. London, 1853, 8vo. Hogarth, Smollett, and Fielding, pp. 219-268.

174. Tuckerman, Bayard, A History of English Prose Fiction from Sir Thomas Malory to George Eliot. New York, 1882, 8vo. Smollett, pp. 211-217.

175. Tytler, A. F., Lord Woodhouselee, Essay on the principles of Translation. Third edition. Edinburgh, 1813, 8vo. Comparison of the translation of Don Quixote by Motteux with that by Smollett, pp. 281-319.

176. Vane, Lady, A letter to the Right Honourable the Lady V____ ss V____, occasioned by the publication of her Memoirs in the "Adventures of Peregrine Pickle." London, 1751, 8vo.

Wershoven, F. J., Smollett et Lesage. 177.
Berlin, 1883, 8vo.

Wilkes, John, The Correspondence of John 178.
Wilkes. 5 vols. London, 1805, 12mo.
Letters of Dr. Smollett to Mr. Wilkes,
vol. i., pp. 49-51.

Wilson, Daniel, Memorials of Edinburgh in the 179.
Olden Time. Edinburgh, 1872, 4to.
References to Smollett.

    Reminiscences of Old Edinburgh. 180.
2 vols. Edinburgh, 1878, 8vo.
References to Smollett.

Magazine Articles

"Tobias George Smollett," Quarterly Review, 181.
vol. 103, 1858, pp. 66-108; same
article, Littell's Living Age, vol. 56,
pp. 641-695. Gentleman's Magazine,
by George B. Smith, vol. 14, N.S., 1875,
pp. 729-737.

"   at Chelsea." London Magazine, by 182.
T. H. Gibson, vol. 2, 1876, pp. 98-103.

"   at Nice." Macmillan's Magazine, by 183.
W. J. Prowse, vol. 21, 1870, pp. 527-533.

"   Count Fathom." Monthly Review, 184.
vol. 8, 1753, pp. 203-214.

"   History of England." Monthly Review, 185.
vol. 16, 1757, pp. 530-536; vol. 18, 1758,
pp. 289-305; vol. 28, 1763, pp. 249-256,
359-369. Critical Review, vol. 3, 1757,
pp. 449-458, 81-499; vol. 5, 1758, pp. 1-17.

"   Inedited Memorials of." Atlantic 185.
Monthly, by W. Sargent, vol. 3, pp. 693-703.

"   Life and Writings of." London Maga- 186.
zine, vol. 6, 1822, pp. 327-335; same

Smollett Bibliography   229

" article, Portfolio, vol. 15, fourth series, 1823, pp. 89-105.

187. " _____ Memoir of." Museum of Foreign Literature, vol. 5, p. 209, etc.

188. " _____ The Regicide." Monthly Review, vol. 1, 1749, pp. 72-79.

189. " _____ Sterne and Fielding." Portfolio, vol. 6, N.S., 1811, pp. 412-431. Gentleman's Magazine, by Charles Cowden Clarke, vol. 8, N.S., 1872, pp. 556-580.

190. " _____ Translation of Don Quixote." Monthly Review, vol. 13, 1755, pp. 196-202.

191. " _____ Translation of Voltaire's Works." Monthly Review, vol. 29, 1763, pp. 273-282.

192. " _____ Travels through France and Italy." Monthly Review, vol. 34, 1766, pp. 419-429.

VIII. Chronological List of Works

193. 1746   Advice, a Satire

194. 1747   Reproof, a Satire (Sequel to Advice).

195. 1748   Adventures of Roderick Random

196. 1749   The Regicide, a Tragedy

197.   Adventures of Gil Blas (Trans.)

198. 1751   Adventures of Peregrine Pickle

199. 1752   Essay on the External Use of Water

200. 1753   Adventures of Ferdinand, Count Fathom

201. 1755   History and Adventures of Don Quixote (Trans.)

202. 1756, etc.   The Critical Review (Edited)

1756	Compendium of authentic and entertaining Voyages (Edited.)	203.
1757	The Reprisal, a Comedy	204.
1757-58	Complete History of England	205.
1763-65	Continuation of do.	206.
1759-66	Modern part of an Universal History (Contributed)	207.
1760-67	The British Magazine (Edited)	208.
1761, etc.	Works of Voltaire (Trans.)	209.
1762-3	The Briton (Edited)	210.
1762	Adventures of Sir Launcelot Greaves	211.
1764	The Present State of all Nations	212.
1766	Travels through France and Italy	213.
1769	History and Adventures of an Atom	214.
1771	The Expedition of Humphry Clinker	215.
1773	Ode to Independence	216.
1776	The Adventures of Telemachus (Trans.)	217.